River for My Sidewalk

GILEAN DOUGLAS

1984
Sono Nis Press
Victoria, British Columbia

Copyright © 1984 Gilean Douglas

Canadian Cataloguing in Publication Data

Douglas, Gilean.
  River for my sidewalk
  ISBN 0-919203-41-8
  1. Douglas, Gilean. 2. Natural history—British Columbia. 3. Naturalists—British Columbia—Biography. 4. Outdoor life—British Columbia. I. Title.
  QH106.2.B7D69 1984   574.9711   C84-091363-X

First edition published
October 1953 by J. M. DENT & SONS
(Canada) Ltd.
Copyright © 1953 by Grant Madison

This edition published by
SONO NIS PRESS
1745 Blanshard Street
Victoria, British Columbia
Canada V8W 2J8

Designed, printed and bound in Canada by
MORRISS PRINTING COMPANY LTD.
Victoria, British Columbia

*For Jürg and Leo,
true friends of happy days.*

Contents

A Way of Life	11
As Wild as They Make It	16
At Home in the Universe	22
How to Live Without Money	27
Visiting the Hard Way	32
Mad as a March Bear	37
Grandpa is a Gentleman	40
Soliloquy in Strawberries	46
Personality Plural	49
Spring Cleaning	54
Pioneering Isn't *That* Easy	57
Crazy Like a Canoe	61
Strangers of the Earth	65

Wilderness Love Story	68
Insurance for Living	73
Cabin Bogey Man	79
Wilderness Wayfarers	83
December Garden	89
Merry Christmas to All	94
Wilderness Welcome	99
Logic out of Eden	104
January Jaunt	108
Moon of the Great Cold	114
February Fires	119
February Footnotes	124
Wings in my Valley	128

Acknowledgements

Thanks are due to *The Vancouver Sun*, *The Northern Sportsman*, *The Land*, *Boy's Life*, *The Villager* (U.S.), *Free Press Weekly*, *Forest and Outdoors*, *Emerald Empire Magazine* (U.S.), *Canadian Nature*, *Country Guide*, *Family Herald and Weekly Star* and *The Countryman* (England) for permission to reprint in this book essays which first saw the light of day in their pages.

A Way of Life

A GREAT deal is being written and said these days about "the Canadian way of life." But there is not just one method of Canadian living, there are a hundred or more. They share the heredity of freedom, but it is environment which shapes and changes them. They grow old and are pushed back into the chimney corner by a new generation of scientific discoveries or political ideas. They gradually dim in our memories and when we do think of them it is often with surprise that they could ever have existed. Many of us find it impossible to imagine any way of life which is different from the one we know now. Often we are too absorbed in the new to record the passing of the old.

Friends say to me: "Yes, there must be people who are interested in those wilderness stories of yours or they wouldn't sell so well, but why don't you write about things most of us know: cities, science, politics, sports?"

My answer is always the same: "Because you *do* know them. Because there are a thousand writers explaining those things, but only a handful to tell about my way of living. It will soon be gone. I must write about it now so we shall not forget."

Yes, it will soon be gone. The population of the earth is

increasing and the wilderness is shrinking. As the necessity to produce becomes greater and our lives more and more regulated by government, it will be impossible for anyone to do as I have done: make an old miner's shack of 1860 into a comfortable home and live almost entirely off the country.

Everyone in the new world will have to produce something more practical than a few vegetables, some wilderness stories and a growth of soul. Probably most of the people who live then will find that crowded, ordered existence quite natural, for they will be products of the new age. But perhaps there will be some who will look up at the morning sky and wonder what it would be like to live always so close to nature that it is possible to hear the beating of earth's primeval heart.

I can tell them what it is like. It is the most wonderful thing that could ever happen to anyone. The hours in my Cascade mountain valley don't run by time clock or whistle; they are regulated much more grandly by the sun and moon. I get up at daylight and I go to bed at dark. If the moon happens to be bright before dawn arrives I get up then and steal a march on the day. I do own a clock, but I only look at it when I have to go "outside" or have promised to have a meal with one of my neighbours. Whether there is Daylight Saving or not makes no difference to me. It is not the regulated hour which is important, but the great simplicity of light.

The boss of my work is the weather. If it is fine then brush cutting, garden work, irrigation, expeditions for flower specimens, bird notes and photographs are the order of the day. If it rains then that is just the time to write, weed, hunt slugs or do the thousand and one workshop jobs which always seem to be ready and waiting for a rainy interlude. When snow covers the earth I shovel long paths to root house and river, saw and split my year's supply of wood, read and contemplate. All weather is good because there is always something good to be done. All time is good—but there is never enough of it for all the things I want to do. Yes, that I *want* to do. I cannot remember performing one task here that I did not thoroughly enjoy.

"Task - work"—they seem such strange words to apply to what I am doing. Anyone who knows what I accomplish here knows also that I work hard and long, yet all that I do is not work but delight. I even enjoy getting up in the morning. Who wouldn't if her alarm clock was the beautiful song of the hermit thrush, repeated over and over from a stump just outside the bedroom window? If the sun made a field of cloth of gold on high peaks and strode through the forest like an army with banners? If one could draw the precious air of freedom deep, deep into lungs and feel it quickening the heart until it wanted to shout for joy?

The day is my friend. I meet it with outstretched hand and use every moment of it to the utmost. Sitting in the house I have partially built I eat the food which I have grown for myself. I have tried to learn everything there is to know about the trees, flowers, birds, animals, insects and rocks which are all around me. It has taken me years and will take more years, but I feel that every grain of such knowledge brings me closer to the great harvest of the universe.

The night is my love. Dusk comes with the benediction of the thrush and the darkening of river water. The clearing is all shadow and the forest dim with mystery. The shade climbs higher and higher up the mountains which ring my valley, leaving only the peaks crested with sunlight. Everything becomes slower and more silent as the dusk deepens into night. Then stars burn silver in the sky and sometimes the moon sails a midnight sea to a port beyond the tall evergreens of Home Wood. This has been the way of night in the wilderness for untold eons. How few living now have ever known it as I do! Campers, fishermen, hunters come in here bringing their shouts and drinking and luxuries. They go home to boast of their wilderness adventures, but all they take away is a paste jewel in a plastic setting.

Little has changed here since this junction of the Teal and Wren rivers was first discovered by explorers thrusting out into unknown regions from the overland trails of the fur brigade. Coyotes still chase the mule deer, black bears still scoop ants from rotting logs, cougars still ambush the unwary grouse and scream through the mountain darkness. But there are few mink, otters or wolverines now, and the beaver is almost extinct. There are not many great trees left; only their stumps to remind us that giants once lived in this land. But the rivers still run singing from the hills with trout flashing in the greenstone-coloured water. Fir, hemlock and cedar—some of them two or three hundred years old—still crowd the forest, with willow, aspen and alder marching beside the streams. It is still possible to look in any direction and not see even a curl of smoke; to live the whole winter through—and most of the rest of the year—without sight or sound of a human being.

Many of us are or have been prospectors, placer or hard rock miners. That way of life is fast disappearing also. Soon there will be no one to recount the sagas of the gold hunters who trudged through searing deserts or ran white mountain water in dugout canoes. There will be no one to spice the histories of our present cities with roaring tales of their mining camp beginnings. The silver towns will fall into dust and there will be no one to revive them with legend and anecdote.

The modern prospector hunts the minerals of war and

peace by plane and frequently comes back to civilization each night for his apple pie with ice cream. He has all the resources of this Age of Machines behind him. He can be reasonably sure that he will never spend his last days in a mountain cabin, packing dudes and panning gold each summer rather than take an old age pension—but happy as only that man can be who has a simple life, his own special brand of happiness and liberty bounded only by the rights of his neighbour.

All this is going—going. Let me tell of it now.

As Wild as They Make It

WHEN in Vancouver I say: "I'm going home," I mean that I'm taking a train to a dark brown patch in the Cascade Mountains that turns out to be a shed and a couple of shacks. That's the easy part of the journey. From there, shank's mare has to take me and my supplies up a mountain, down the other side and through half a mile of fairly level forest land to the banks of the Teal River.

That's when I shift to cage and cable for the last lap of the trip. There are not many of these conveyances left, but there used to be quite a few of them wherever prospectors set up more or less permanent camps or trappers had their main cabins. I have photographed them on the Rio Grande, the Rogue, the Feather, the Sacramento and many lesser streams. The only other one I know about in this part of British Columbia is a couple of mountains away from me and belongs to a Canadian outdoor writer who would boot me headfirst down an otter slide if I mentioned his name when I'm talking so close to home!

It is a well-known fact that all trains arrive at whistle stops in the middle of the night and ours is no exception. In the rains of autumn or the heavy snows of winter this trudge over part of the Cascade Range with "bug" or flashlight is something my very few, hand-picked visitors will never forget. But from March to October it's the most beautiful walk I've ever taken. Sometimes you do the whole thing in daylight; at others you watch the black velvet of night change to the grey chiffon of dawn and finally to the gold brocade of full sunlight. The scent of wet earth and conifer needles is in your nostrils and usually there's a breeze blowing down from the peaks that has the perfume of hyacinth in it, no matter what time of year it happens to be. But it isn't hyacinth, it's wet bracken and you can smell it most strongly at the beginning and end of winter.

From what the records tell us, British Columbia came out from under its ice blanket only about ten thousand years ago and so its flora and fauna are still in a pretty fluid state. Logging, forest fires, human habitation and destruction of beaver have changed the country a great deal. Streams have dried up, spring floods are greater, there are fewer water ouzels and the number of fruit-eating birds has increased considerably. The steeper mountain sides, bared by fire and axe, have felt the skeleton hand of erosion laid along their flanks. Moss-lichen is the rule with them now and their bright brooks sing only in spring and fall. This is the story—and worse—wherever we go on this earth of ours which was once so balanced and so beautiful.

Where I live was originally primeval conifer forest and I believe it is for this reason that many botanists and ornithologists have the idea that it is very low in bird and plant life. I was told before I went in that I would find very little variety in either. After two years I had a record of 97 bird species— which has since been considerably increased—and 189 flower varieties. I am quite sure this record could be appreciably bettered by someone with more knowledge and experience—

but they would not have an easy task. By this I mean that the country is so rugged, the devil's club and salmonberry brush so tenacious—not to mention thick alder growth to be hacked through and streams to be forded—that it requires much time and muscularity to wrest any secrets at all from such a wild land. There is heavy ground cover almost everywhere with Oregon grape, willow, spiraea, western dogwood and several varieties of berries accounting for a lot of it. Down timber is all over the place and this, combined with the heavy undergrowth, makes forests that the fishermen and hunters term impenetrable and that we call aggravating.

The evergreens consist principally of western hemlock, red cedar and Douglas fir, with grand and amabalis fir, yew, Sitka spruce, yellow cypress, white pine and a bit of western birch. Actually I have no living birch around me, except the mountain variety which grows higher up the slopes with mountain hemlock, Rocky Mountain and dwarf juniper, Engelmann's spruce, alpine fir and lodgepole pine. The deciduous trees along my two rivers are the black cottonwood, red alder, broadleaved and vine maple, with several varieties of willow: Hooker's, longleaf and black willow are the kinds closest to my cabin. Farther up the mountains I have come across Barclay's and Arctic willow with the Sitka alder and mountain ash.

There are, however, tracts which are almost primeval still: great trees, practically no underbrush, much moss. These are very beautiful places and after coming across them I was not surprised to find that the insect-eating birds of the primitive conifer forests were still very much in evidence. These include my year-round neighbour, the winter wren, and Maestro, the hermit thrush, who doubles as my summer alarm clock. The startling pileated woodpecker, the silent pigmy owl, busy

Townsend and black-throated grey warblers come under this heading also, together with kinglets, nuthatches, flycatchers and chickadees. Cut-over and burned areas have brought in other birds: the white-crowned and song sparrows, Oregon junco, black-headed grosbeak, Townsend solitaire (my hermit-minded friend), grouse, jay, robin, mountain bluebird, red-shafted flicker and yellow warbler among them.

Poised as I am between wet and dry belts—with the accent on the dry side—I feel that I have an almost perfect climate. My only complaint is that, because of the high mountains around me, I never see either a sunrise or a sunset—only the after effects of both. Also, the sun leaves my glen in late October and I don't glimpse it again until the end of January and then only for a few moments between gaps in the hills. But all this only makes me appreciate more the sunny, showery days of spring and the bright almost rainless days of summer.

At the beginning of March there may still be several feet of snow on the ground, but by the end of the month I am planting. By May—and certainly by June—I am irrigating and this keeps on well into September. Autumns are glorious. The hills shout with colour until the first frosts arrive in mid-October. Then there is usually a period of rain, although sometimes we plunge from warm-hearted Indian summer right into winter. But even winter is not very hard on us. The snow may be five or six feet deep—three times that in the mountains—but the temperature rarely drops below zero and usually hovers around 12 to 16 degrees above. The woods close to my cabin are so dense that there is seldom more than two feet of snow, if that, on the trails. By March such a hard crust has formed that you can walk anywhere without sinking or can put a chair and table on top of it to write in the warm sunshine, as I do.

All winter long the water ouzels—usually called dippers—do setting-up exercises on the stones of the Wren, the kingfisher shrieks from his perch on the cable over the Teal, wren and mountain chickadee sample my free lunch, kinglets sample the cedars and the great grey owl is a deeper shadow of the dusk. The varied thrush—called "rainpiper" here, although I can assure you that he neither conjures up downpours nor prophesies them correctly—goes deeper into the forest in his shyness. Tracks of black bear, lynx, cougar, coyote, mink, fisher, marten, wolverine, weasel, rock rabbit, mouse, shrew and pack rat signature the snow—but there is seldom a deer print. The coyotes and cougars have almost wiped them out. Sometimes a grizzly drifts in from farther east, a porcupine investigates my axe handle or a skunk family takes up temporary residence. Higher up the mountains golden and bald eagles soar above mountain goats, the marmot gives his warning whistle and the white-tailed ptarmigan plays invisible.

Spring comes in with a rush of foaming rivers, bursting buds, chattering squirrels and mating songs. Canada geese cry over; harlequin, merganser and goldeneye go up the streams to nest; sapsuckers and woodpeckers zoom across my clearing; the song birds return to their old territories and tell the world about it. Juncos and sparrows almost push me off the doorstep trying to get at the bread crumbs and oatmeal. Sometimes western and eared grebes say a short "hello" or a yellow-headed blackbird (who is not supposed to be here at all) flirts a wing in passing. An osprey flies majestically down the Teal, vaux swifts monogram the air, calliope and rufous hummingbirds give me indignant looks because the window boxes aren't out yet. More birds seem to arrive every moment and I have visions of a jammed flyway with rear-end collisions.

In the summer the prospectors come in: fresh from the mining school in Vancouver and rarin' to go. That is just about as far as they get, for although it is still possible to pan coarse gold and a little platinum in my two rivers there is hardly enough of either to be worth the trouble. But it wasn't always this way. The old trails which cross my clearing or wind beyond it saw many a lucky prospector in the years following 1858. They made history, those trails. They were pungent with sweat and loud with oaths. Now they are scented with syringa and leaf-mould while only the silver song of birds breaks their green silence.

Timber is the gold of the wilds now. The more accessible parts of my district have been cut over and there is a big logging company eyeing it again, but they are going to have an expensive job getting the best stuff out. My own small holding I shall keep inviolate. Meanwhile I watch a flock of black swifts whirl through a canyon like small, dark leaves as I climb to where I know one of three lovely rein orchids can be found. Rosy finch and pipit watch my ascent, a Clark's crow gives raucous greeting and a red-tailed hawk slants down through the alpine sun. A waterfall bordered with mist maidens plunges down a cliff, blue-eyed grass and lupine bring heaven to a meadow and suddenly a horned lark spurns even these six thousand feet of height for thinner, freer air. Four thousand feet below me is my home: hand-hewn and small, but as much a part of the wilderness as though it had root-sprung from this Jurassic ground—and I with it.

At Home in the Universe

I LIVE IN a wilderness valley of the Cascade Mountains with my nearest neighbour four bush miles away and the nearest city well over a hundred. I live on fish, a little wild meat, wild berries and plants of hill and forest, vegetables from my own garden. The material self-sufficiency which I have known here for years has revitalized my city-bred mentality almost unbelievably.

I can remember the slow growth of that feeling during my first year in the valley and its final flowering when I had proved to myself that I could build my own home, fashion my own tools and buy all the food I needed with the coins of patience, work and ingenuity. You would have laughed to see how I gloated over my full wood-shed, the loaded shelves of my root house, the cedar shake panelling of my walls. It was all so new and so good. During the years since then there has been perpetual thanksgiving in my heart for these things and it will never cease until I do.

But I found that material self-sufficiency was not enough. I needed to be self-sufficient spiritually as well. You will understand that when I use the term "self-sufficient" I realize that none of us can ever really be that. We are all dependent upon something or someone to a greater or a lesser degree. Yet that term is the best one I know to describe what I mean.

You will often hear it said that individuals who live alone in an isolated place become "bushed" in time. Like all sweeping statements this one is only partly true. Some people do and some do not. The ones who don't are the ones who are independent spiritually. They don't need a clutter of things or a clatter of people to be happy. They can make companions out of trees, music out of rivers, laughter out of the antics of their furred and feathered neighbours—and inspiration out of everything. They feel at home in the universe.

I am convinced that one reason why people get "bushed" is because they are told they will. They have had it drummed into them for so long that they must have people, they must have radios, they must have newspapers, they must have change that they not only believe it, they make it true—for themselves at least. Another reason is that you have to acquire some of the good old-fashioned virtues before you can live satisfactorily with yourself in the universe. People who liked to live by themselves weren't always considered strange, you know. Pioneers and explorers—who certainly had to be isolated for long stretches of time—were admired, hermits were venerated and it was taken as a matter of course that great prophets should come out of the wilderness. But not today! From the time we are toddlers we are trained to have social consciousness, to adapt ourselves to our environment, to adjust, adjust, adjust. Adjust to what? To other people. That's splendid and I agree with it, but it doesn't go far enough. I have never had any difficulty adjusting to others and I could take my environment or leave it alone, but when I came into the mountains I had a pretty hard time learning to adjust to myself. That was something I hadn't been taught.

There had always been layers of speech, activity and the printed word interposed between myself and me. I didn't know how to think; I didn't know how to be independent either materially or spiritually and I freely confess that I never had such difficulty getting along with anyone as I did with myself.

But I soon learned. I had to. One of the first things I noticed was that after a few weeks my mind and body were steadier and calmer than they had ever been. My thoughts became more ordered and comprehensive; I saw things more in whole and less in biased part. My senses and my powers of imagination and inventiveness were quickened immeasurably. I became both more philosophical and lighter of heart. Without the constant pressure of people and events, freed from the eternal noise and propaganda of modern living, I developed a gaiety of mind that I had never known before—and I have always been a happy person. History wasn't snapping at my heels any more for I had discovered universal happenings which would have made the didoes of earth seem ridiculous if they hadn't been so tragic for so many.

It is amazing how few people can work or eat properly while they are alone. If they have company then no one gallops through the day's work better then they, but left to themselves they dawdle and shirk and seem to lose all interest in what they are trying to accomplish. This means, of course, that they have never learned self-discipline and the joy of working for work's sake. Poor souls, what they have missed! Self-discipline is also needed when it comes to good meals at regular hours. I don't know how many men and women living alone, either temporarily or permanently, have said to me:

"Oh, I just can't be bothered to cook anything decent. I

just get myself some tea and bread when I feel hungry."

No wonder they go a bit daft eventually! The strangest ideas go round as to what artists and other people who don't punch time clocks do with their time. The ones I know work like fury and yet they never, never manage to do all they want to. The days are far too short, the weeks seem to telescope into each other, the years go by like greased lightning. I am up at dawn and it's a queer day that hasn't at least twelve hours of work in it. One reason I consider myself so lucky is that I can work as long and hard as I choose without anyone being upset or thinking I am heading for a lunatic asylum. Of course, I can shift from mental to physical work and back again whenever I feel the need. If I were putting in nut No. 17859 every day I would probably be all for shorter hours so that I would have more time for work outdoors or at something creative. Which brings us to square pegs in round holes, the use of leisure, outlets for the creative urge—and enough material for another book.

It is easy to see why dictators make noise, perpetual motion and mob scenes part of their programs. That is the way to divorce people from that great revolutionary, thought. Modern life itself does a pretty good job of that. I am so glad that I know what is outside that noisy, smoky room; that I have been able to step out into sunlight and feel the cool, free wind in my hair. That I have been able to fulfil at least a small part of what I believe to be the true destiny of man: to live up to the highest in himself and to become a citizen of the universe.

It is, I know, quite impossible for most people to do as I have done, to live as I live. They have dependants, or obligations or else they could not endure a life which would seem to them to consist of nothing but isolation, poverty and work. But it is not impossible for each of us, wherever we are, to make a little oasis of quiet in the hurly-burly of living. How can we get to know anyone—God, ourselves, the people around us—if we never take time to really contemplate them? How can we find out where we are going and why and if we are on the right road for us? How can we hear the "music of the spheres" without silence or grow soul without solitude? In that oasis of quiet we can be kings and there each one can learn to rule his most rebellious subject—himself.

How to Live Without Money

WHEN the varied thrush calls from the forest and there is that feeling of waiting quietness over my valley which always precedes the spring, I begin to long for the perfume of spaded soil and the flower-scent of wet bracken which has been touched by the returning sun. Working out my garden-to-be on paper, I have that splendid feeling of material self-sufficiency which is such a vital part of wilderness life. If all the stores closed and all the railroads stopped running I could still manage. I know, for I have done just that.

Except for me the wild strawberries of the district go unpicked, the Oregon grapes ungathered. I have been told repeatedly that red elderberries, black nightshade and the berries of star flower, false Solomon's seal, twisted stalk and fairy bells are poisonous. Well, I have eaten them all and am still very much alive.

The Chinese would be appalled at my neighbours who order in crates of fruit while leaving that on the wild bushes outside their doors to wither. The famines which have tortured China for centuries did one good thing: they forced people to make use of every palatable plant—and probably a good many that weren't. This was the only way that inhabitants of districts cut off by mountain ranges or rivers in flood could hope to keep alive until help arrived or a catch crop ripened. The records of these edible discoveries can be found in Famine Herbals such as the Chiu Huang Pen Ts'ao by Chou Ting-wang, the fifth son of the first Ming Emperor, who lived about 500 years ago. Chou Ting-wang was not content with having these herbs pointed out to him by country folk and hermits, but he had them brought into his garden and planted there for observation. He wrote descriptions of each one and commissioned artists to make paintings of them. Still not satisfied, he divided them into groups according to whether their leaves, blossoms, roots or stalks were edible and published the result in 1406.

Because of this and other Famine Herbals, deficiency diseases caused by lack of minerals or vitamins are virtually unknown to the Chinese, even to those of exceedingly low incomes. This was true before the Second World War, at least. There is little reason to doubt that the Chinese of ancient times made use of ingredients for body nourishment which we as yet know little or nothing about. Before the war a Chinese who could spend as little as ten cents a day on food could keep well, thanks to the dietary practices handed down to him by his ancestors.

Before I knew about such Oriental eating habits I had been getting along on approximately ten cents a day myself and by the same methods. To start at the end, I had fruit desserts growing all over the place: wild raspberries, blackberries, black currants, swamp currants, high and low bush cranberries, black caps, salmonberries, red and blue huckleberries, red and blue elderberries, mountain blueberries, saskatoons, thimbleberries (better cooked than fresh), black gooseberries, wild cherries, blue currants, swamp gooseberries, western teaberries and the ones I have mentioned before. Maybe I've even left out a few! There were hazelnuts to eat with my dandelion root coffee or one of my many wilderness teas: Labrador, elderflower, firewood, mint, sage, ginger, clover, violet, camomile, snowberry, strawberry and plantain.

Salads presented no problem for I could use these: sorrel, dandelion, mustard, lamb's quarters, onion, plantain, shepherd's purse, horsetail, clover and, most delicious of all, miner's lettuce. Dinner's main course could be steelhead, Dolly Varden or rainbow trout from my rivers, or, if I wanted to save up my dimes for ammunition, I could feast on venison, grouse or mountain goat in season—or bear at any time. I could set willow snares for rabbits—except that they've been so meticulous about never coming on my property that I wouldn't have the heart to go out trapping them unless I were starving. I might as well break down and confess right here—to the horror of all gun-toting sportsmen—that I'd almost as soon take a pot-shot at some of my human neighbours as I would at the animals I've mentioned. I've done it—at the animals, I mean!—but not since I came to live in my valley and probably not again unless it's a case of them or me. The animals I've met here have been mighty decent and I'd like to return the compliment.

Such ideas have practically made me a vegetarian. That's an easy thing to be in the wilderness for everywhere you go you stumble over plants that can be used as pot herbs or green vegetables, onions, of course—and nettles are almost as well known—plus all the salads I mentioned above, which are as good cooked as raw.

The first spring shoots of yellow arum make one of my favourite vegetables, coming as they do after long months of root eating.

But these roots are not to be despised. Those of yellow arum can be ground into flour (hard to come by in the wilderness) or baked in the oven. The Indians used to roast them in pits together with scrapings of inner hemlock bark. It takes a long time to do it that way but the result is worth it. Wild clover roots are even better—especially when you dip them in fish oil—and those of the Yampah (a plant of the fennel family) are best of all. Yampah is good eaten fresh, boiled, roasted, dried, baked or fried in oil, but I used to have a hard time beating the squirrels to it. Yellow lily bulbs are delicious, but the one I sampled is the last I'll ever dig up, for this beautiful wildflower is being picked to extinction. Lupine (not harmful to human beings as it is to animals) and columbine roots are said to be all right, but I haven't tried them and I didn't care much for those of mountain dock. The edible thistle does a double turn, for its roots are delicious baked and they can also be used as a sugar substitute. The Indians used to get sugar from the dew which collected on milkweed flowers, but I'm not patient enough for that. Shield fern roots are tasty and the rhizomes make a good green. The sap wood of young lodgepole pine or aspen makes a nice change in diet. Young shoots of salmonberry, thimbleberry and fireweed are fine too.

Additional flour can be obtained from bracken roots, while extract of juniper berries would have been just the thing for A. A. Milne's butterless King. Butter was a bit of a problem in my dime days, but I found that I didn't miss it much anyway. Fish oil seemed to supply the necessary fats and when my neighbours traded me food for labour I was all set. I became quite fond of pemmican—berries mixed with fat or meat and made into cakes—and I could quite see why it was the standby of Indians and explorers. There were probably a number of food plants that I never discovered and, of course, each district has its own or—as on the coast—additional varieties. However, I was tucking away a nice assortment of amino acids, minerals and vitamins—with the accent on vitamin C which I drank in rose hip syrup or ate in a salad of wood sorrel leaves. I was lean as a lath, but healthy as they come and I could turn out a day's work that would give most people nightmares. Just for the fun of it, I had a medical checkup afterwards and the result would have satisfied even Tarzan.

I have a sneaking suspicion that I've never been quite as well since. Now I have a garden, fruit trees and I import flour, sugar, rolled oats, meat, milk and margarine. If I were able to grow soy beans I could eliminate the meat easily and I have never been able to go back whole-heartedly to regulation tea and coffee. I get a lot of my sweetening from sugar beets and all my flavourings except salt, pepper and a few tropical spices come out of my herb bed. Like Chou Ting-wang I have most of the wild foods growing in my valley now and I sometimes wonder why I don't make up a modern Herbal for a generation which seems to be suffering from a famine of ideas, intitiative and independence.

Visiting the Hard Way

SUMMER OR winter those who live in the country can expect to have their time and food neatly eroded by trickles, streams and floods of visitors. There is no doubt in my mind that the first paying guest originated in the bright brain of a country dweller who decided to get more than work and worry out of these invasions.

I, however, although also a householder in the great outdoors, am in a unique position. I can usually handpick all the human visitors who come to my home. I say "usually" because the two rivers which protect me from intruders are fordable for about six weeks of the year—in late summer and early fall—and during that period anything can happen and usually does. My animal visitors arrive at all hours and seasons, of course, but they are wilderness sourdoughs like myself and so are always welcome.

The guests I invite must have understanding hearts, broad minds and rugged constitutions. Above all they must have a touch of the pioneer spirit and that zest for adventure which seems to burn less and less brightly in these days when every luxury is considered a necessity. I have no electricity, no running water (except in the rivers), no spring-filled mattresses. My meals come out of the streams, the hills, my garden or from the hundreds of wild berry bushes in or near my clearing. As everything has to be packed in on my back or on those of my neighbours—the nearest of whom lives four miles away—my furniture and tools are either homemade or non-existent. To me my cabin is the most comfortable place I've ever lived in—and I've stayed in everything from a palace to a pup-tent—but a lot of people wouldn't agree with me. Certainly it is no place for those who get claustrophobia from tall mountains or who think all dense forests hide man-eating monsters.

Any visitors from outside have to undergo considerable wilderness conditioning before they even arrive at my valley. I am one large mountain and a half a mile of forest away from our whistle-stop station. My guests dash off the train—which barely hesitates—with a wild look of wonder in their eyes as to whether they have actually arrived at the right place. Usually they are well equipped for the trail (I don't invite anyone who isn't part mountain goat) and after I have picked up any mail or express we get under way without too much difficulty. Our greatest trouble is pulling loose from those sleepless neighbours whose houses bubble with tea and curiosity. In summer we usually succumb to the former because if we wait around a while we can walk over the mountain in daylight.

The trail is straight and fairly level for a quarter of a mile, then it goes up and a long way down by a series of switchbacks. These are often a maze to the alien foot and I begin to feel like a cowboy on the Last Roundup. In summer they offer no difficulty to a good walker, but after a deluge of rain—either frozen or unfrozen—they are as slick as glass and anyone carrying a heavy pack has two strikes against him. If he goes down his only hope is to crawl to a tree and pull himself up by it. Let me say here that a packboard is far better for a long trail than any pack ever invented. It puts the weight where you can take it and doesn't bounce against your vertebrae with every step.

Except on moonlight nights the darkness of these mountain woods is definitely Stygian. Occasionally it is broken by the glow of eyes parallelling our course. These belong to the most curious of all my neighbours, the wildcats and cougars. When I tell my guests that these nocturnal nomads are harmless they look considerably less than convinced. After such a contretemps I notice them gazing around a bit nervously when a branch cracks or a rock rolls down the mountain, while the scream of a rock rabbit sometimes brings on a mild case of the jitters. Fortunately none of them have heard a cougar scream!

When we reach the foot of the switchback there is a new sound, one which is felt rather than heard. It becomes louder and louder as we walk along the narrow trail with great firs, hemlocks and cedars stretching away on either side. In spring and autumn it is a crashing, roaring symphony which seems to fill the whole forest. In summer and winter it is the legato accompaniment to a primeval night. To me it is my welcome home.

I have often wished that I could read the minds of some of my guests when they arrive at the source of this wild music and see the spray of that swift mountain river, the Teal, flashing white against the blackness of night and deep water. Surely some of the awe an explorer feels when coming upon an unknown wilderness stream must touch them then. But when they realize that they must climb a sixteen-foot homemade ladder to a frail platform part way up a giant fir and suspended over this raging torrent, their expressions show distinctly modified delight. The platform has no railing, so you can step off into space quite easily—but there is really no good reason to do so. The cage—two wide boards fastened by wires to roller bearings running on a thick wire rope—swings there, held to the tree by a looped wire and hook. It will accommodate two passengers with packs or three without luggage, and it tips easily around the edges. I've lost a trout and a chocolate cake that way, but never a guest.

The first passengers get on board and grip the cable above them with both hands to keep the cage from starting ahead of schedule after it is unhooked and before the last passenger can leap aboard. Then away we go, sliding easily and swiftly along the cable through the darkness with one small lantern swinging at our prow. It is quite a thrill for those who think all transportation began with the motor car. But from this side—where the platform is considerably higher than the home landing—it is a quick, easy ride through the night. The pull uphill coming back will take longer and be harder work. This arrangement works well, however, as the biggest loads come in and anyone who goes "outside" is usually travelling light.

Soon we are climbing the stone steps to my clearing and going down the path to where my cabin makes a deeper shadow against the darkness of forest and mountain. In summer daylight, with the birds singing matins and the garden in full summer bloom, my guests exclaim with amazement and delight. But when we arrive in this gloom and, except for the rivers, silence; when they can sense the wildness and solitude all around them, then they are very quiet—wondering, possibly, why on earth they ever accepted my invitation.

Uninvited human visitors seldom get to my cabin at all; either because I don't like their looks and so don't unhook the cage for them or because they think getting on such a contraption would be certain death. This latter decision suits us both for my valley is definitely no place for the fainthearted. Some years the river is never low enough to ford at all and then I can bask in unsocial isolation. When it shrinks to knee-depth I resign myself to receiving all comers. These range from sourdough prospectors—for whom the welcome mat is always out—to girls in high-heel shoes and not much else who shriek at all my little garter snakes and scare them into spasms. How some of these people ever manage to get this far is a mystery, but I notice that only my hand-picked guests and veterans of the woods ever come back again.

Mad as a March Bear

Now I'm not asking you to believe this; I didn't myself when I saw it. But it just goes to show that March is a crazy month, and the Ides aren't the only things dangerous in it.

The other morning I was going across the river to see if the yellow arum was up in my favourite patch. I was looking forward to my first spring feed on its tender green stalks. Just as I unhooked the cage I remembered that there was a good cedar butt for shakes over there, and that I'd have to re-roof part of the woodshed this year. So I left the cage swinging free—as there isn't enough sag in the cable from the home platform for the cage to slide away by itself when it's empty—and went back to my cabin for sledge hammer and wedges.

When I started down the rockery steps from the knoll on my way back, I spotted the cage about twenty feet along the cable, and said words. The river was high and I'd have to go out on that wire rope hand over hand, and then swing myself on board the contraption. I thought it was empty, of course, but then I discovered there was someone or something black on it. I raced down the steps and across the flat, only to come to a sliding stop when I saw a mama bear right in front of me on the river bank. The black thing on my cage was her cub. His curiosity had put him aboard, and his weight—although he was only the size of two of mama's paws—had sent the cage skittering down the slight incline.

Mama was mad. She was trying to focus her weak eyes—especially weak after hibernation—and woof at the cub to "come down out of that tree." But he couldn't do that unless he was a tightrope walker or a channel swimmer. He just dug in his little claws, and clung while the cage tipped dangerously as his weight shifted. Mama went down the bank and into the water: then she tried to stand upright and get her front paws on the cage. But the current was too swift, and she came down splash with a rolling lurch that nearly threw her off her feet.

So, of course, there was only one thing for me to do; go out on the cable after the cub. I started hand across hand with my weight hanging from the wire rope. Then mama saw me and decided that I had designs on her darling. She made a couple of lunges at my feet, which were well within pawing distance, and after the second one I forgot to be scared and got mad too. I saw her third swipe coming just as I reached the cage, so I kicked her in the snoot—the tenderest part of a bear—and swung on board.

The cub was too frightened to do more than squeak in a distinctly mousy tone. I held him with one hand while I pulled us both back to the home platform with the other. Mama trotted anxiously through the water to the bank, and was waiting to receive us. But she didn't try to paw me again; she was too worried about her offspring. When I pushed the cub off on to the platform she grabbed him and sniffed him all over and then sat right down there and took him in her arms and rocked him.

Craziest thing I have ever seen, and I don't expect you to believe it. I didn't myself until the cub bounced awkwardly off mama's lap and tried to nip my ankle. That was just a moment or two before his brother came sliding down the knoll hill on his fat little tummy—which, I discovered later, was probably full of my tulip bulbs. Mama had evidently been giving him his first lesson in digging.

Grandpa is a Gentleman

I WOULDN'T go so far as to say that I like all animals better than all people, but certainly the majority of the furred fraternity are easier to get along with and a lot more polite. Take Grandpa, for instance—although I don't think anyone ever will.

The first time I became aware that Grandpa was a neighbour of mine was shortly after I'd come into the mountains to live the life of Crusoe. I was clearing land for vegetables and had axed, dug and clawed my way through an acre of salmonberry brush—may its roots wither and its offspring be baar-bitten! By that time I was almost horizontal myself, but with enough strength left to want a strawberry patch.

I picked out a fine spot with southern exposure and figured I'd have that itsy-bitsy piece dug over in a forenoon. Two and a half days later I staggered up the path to the woodshed and put my tools away. That room-size section of land had everything except strawberries: maple roots, salmonberry stringers that went to Hades, boulders—and devil's club.

I don't know whether you've ever met the last-named variety of flora. Where I live it's an eight-foot plant with umbrella leaves, thorns that make you fester where they stab and roots that are beyond any polite words of mine. Even the leaves are armed with daggers—on both sides. I don't wonder that the Indians considered it big medicine and reserved it for their shamans. Nor that a lot of British Columbia Indian folk lore centres around a hero who, when pursued by enemies, throws something prickly behind him that magic changes into a tangle of devil's club—which all the enemies in the world could never, never get through. Its greenish-white flower is nothing to look at, but the great autumn pannicle of brilliant scarlet berries is one of nature's handsomest stop signs. That red standard shouts: "Here I am!"—and there any sensible person isn't.

However, I got that piece of ground dug over just before dark one spring evening. The next morning I was out at daybreak to transplant strawberries from the wild. When I got back with a load of plants, I saw with amazement that their erstwhile smoothly-raked bed was distinctly rumpled. Right across it, from corner to corner, marched the biggest pawprints I'd ever seen. Cougar or grizzly? In those days I couldn't have told you. All I knew was that those were the largest animals in my part of the woods, so it must be one of them. Anyway, it was just dilly. Probably my strawberry bed was right on an aminal runway and I'd never be able to grow anything better than a crop of cuss words. But I couldn't let the plants die, so I put them in.

That day I could have posed as the storied pioneer: breaking wilderness ground while my rifle leaned against a nearby tree. When I went home at night with tools over one shoulder and gun in the crook of my arm I might have been a Thanksgiving poster. I said thanks next morning all right, when I saw that my newly-planted bed was untouched. But the same huge tracks crossed another piece that I'd just dug over for rhubarb.

"Maybe his feet are sore and he likes the feel of soft earth," I thought. But I didn't leave the gun at home.

This went on for days. Each newly-raked plot had tracks on it next morning, but as soon as I planted anything there it would be left undisturbed. I boxed one set of prints and kept them until the Ranger came.

"Cougar," he said decisively, "and a big one. Well over eight feet. He's probably that old one that's been around here for years. When they get old they can't hunt, you know, and that's when they're dangerous. If you have any children around here this summer don't let them out in the woods alone."

When summer came I realized I had an audience. You know how you can tell when someone's watching you intently? Well, that's the way I felt when I was working in the garden. I'd turn around suddenly, hoping to glimpse whatever or whoever it was, but nothing seemed to be there except the quiet forest about two hundred feet away. My woodpile for the oil drum heater was at the edge of the woods and gradually I became convinced that the watcher was near it. Then one blisteringly hot day I caught a movement out of the corner of my eye and looked up quickly to spy a tawny form flowing down from the top of my woodpile like swift, brown water. Grandpa was taking to the woods for a little coolth.

Our acquaintance went on in this manner for some time and then in August I went higher up the mountains for berries. Not having any stock, I couldn't think of anything that Grandpa could damage while I was gone. But I needn't have worried. Grandpa went right along. Twice the light of my campfire caught his eyes and once when I was trying to reach a favourite camping spot after dark he parallelled me through the woods. Of course I couldn't *swear* it was Grandpa, but it was certainly a cougar—and why not he? I hadn't the foggiest notion whether he was acting according to Hoyle or stalking me for a feast, but when nothing continued to happen I began to look on him as a slightly pixilated trail companion and to feel quite lonely when he wasn't around.

Apparently he stayed up in the high mountains for I didn't feel him in the neighbourhood of my cabin until late September. It rained heavily one night and the next morning when, as usual, I flung the front door wide open to air the house, I saw Grandpa's paw prints decorating my front porch. I wet my own shoes and made my tracks beside his. They dried at almost the same time. So Grandpa must have been standing right outside my front door when I got out of bed and he heard the cedar springs creaking.

The account of this little episode gave some of my neighbours the jitters and for some time they took turns telling me what I should do about Grandpa. Being human, they thought he ought to be killed. An Indian who wandered by considered a spring trap was the thing and each time he returned he would be all for setting it up. But not I. At one time I was waited on by a white delegation which demanded that I send Grandpa to the happy hunting grounds. They admitted that Grandpa had never done anything to them or even been in their neighbourhood, as far as they knew, but still and all.... Perhaps the real reason was the $15 bounty. Off my property they set their traps for him, but Grandpa wasn't having any. On my land I would have defended the old boy with my little gun if necessary, but it didn't come to that. There were no children for nearly forty miles and then they were in a village. Besides, Grandpa is a gentleman.

When snow was deep on the ground Grandpa did a lot of prowling at the wood's edge and along my trails. He was a regular circuit walker; always following the same route and returning to, appropriately enough, Cougar Mountain the same way. It was easy to see that he knew he didn't have any enemies here. Coming back from a four-mile winter walk to a neighbour's, I found that Grandpa had escorted me at a discreet distance almost to the front door. The next morning, out of sheer curiosity, I backtracked my trail and found that he had chaperoned me home too.

But it was the following summer before I actually saw Grandpa. I had climbed the mountains in May to look for a certain species of rein orchid (*Habenaria leptoceratitis*) and was stepping briskly along a deer trail when something made me look up suddenly. There was Grandpa—now it *could* have been Grandpa!—fading off a rock ledge. But, unlike the Cheshire cat, he did not smile.

Back at two thousand feet once more, I walked out of my little cabin one June morning to go to some placer diggings a couple of miles away. All I had with me was a jack-knife. The tools I needed for placering were on the spot and I seldom carried a gun. Coming to a tree trunk spanning a shallow gully, I was just about to step on it when I got a familiar whiff. I stood still and let my eyes rove first right and then left. Suddenly I froze into even more rigidity. There, in the bottom of the gully and not twenty yards away from me, was a very large cougar. Grandpa! But could I be sure it was Grandpa! I stared at him, fascinated, and he stared back at me with a sleepy look in his yellow eyes. His tail didn't move.

What to do? To go back was as bad as to go forward and I couldn't stand still forever. I put my foot on the log and kept one on Grandpa. (If only I could be certain it was the old boy.) Nothing happened. I took another step and his tail twitched slightly. I froze again. The tail was still. I went forward again and he remained quiescent. By this time I had reached the centre of the log bridge and couldn't keep the cougar in sight any longer without turning my head over my shoulder. If I didn't watch where I was going I'd be down in the gully too—and wouldn't that be palsy-walsy?

Up to this time I had neither looked on myself as a hero nor thought I was a coward, but now I knew that I was definitely the latter. Those last few yards across that log and the walk along the forest trail afterwards are things I shall never forget. I knew what the cold sweat of terror was then. My heart was hammering and I wasn't too sure that my knees weren't going to throw me. I walked on and on in a sort of daze, not able to look back or do anything else but put one foot in front of the other. Nothing happened and nothing happened and suddenly I knew definitely that nothing was going to happen. It had been Grandpa after all. I stopped and took a breath that seemed to come from my boots. My heart slowed back to normal and by the time I reached the diggings I was myself again. On the walk back I trusted to Grandpa's courtesy and he didn't fail me. The gully was empty.

Don't ask my why he was there in the first place or why he behaves as he does at any time. I've learned a lot of nature lore in the years since I came into the mountains, but I haven't learned that. Nor why and how the old boy goes on and on past his allotted span of twenty years. But one thing I do know: I have never had a less troublesome neighbour nor met anyone with a finer sense of the niceties than Grandpa. Long may his paws track and his eyes gleam on my trails.

Soliloquy in Strawberries

THE TIME when spring spills over into summer is a busy season, but even then there is opportunity for considerable thinking and for the untangling of knotty problems. I find that weeding and desuckering my strawberry plants is a great mental stimulus. For one thing it is a long, slow job; for another, the strawberry bed has such a lovely view. The bed stretches across the knoll to Home Wood and overlooks the sweep of the Teal where the Wren pours in. There is a rockery stretching down from it to the lower flat, huckleberry and blackcap bushes semicircle it and a wild cherry tree stands not far away.

The snows melt there first and in autumn the very last rays of the departing sun strike down on it. I always seem to find a good excuse for working out there in the cold ground of October, with the valley dark and chill around me, just when the sun flashes into the gap for its five or ten minute's stay. Off goes my windbreaker and I turn up my face so as not to miss a single ray. In that one place everything is warm and bright, but if I go even a few steps towards the cabin I feel as though I had stepped from day into night.

It is the same in February, when excuses for being out there in the snow are a little harder to find. But in spring and summer it is a warm, glowing place looking down a valley and river bed of light. It is also one of the busiest spots in the garden then, for both weeds and suckers seem to grow there with diabolical speed. I go up and down the rows of half an acre, but my thoughts travel the world. I always begin by thinking how lucky I am to be there at all; that leads to cogitations on my favourite thesis of the benefits of silence and solitude—and I'm over the hills and far away!

Last winter I read several books on medieval themes and I was impressed by the many references in them to "retreats" and "hours of quietude." The churchmen of old days had special cubicles into which those who were overwrought or under tension could go for calming contemplation. "Going into the silences" was not considered mystical or odd in those times. It was accepted as a necessary and natural part of the balanced life. Those who practised it had no particular name for themselves or for what they advocated, although we moderns might term the latter either instinct or psychology. Actually, they simply recognized a fact and provided what it called for. They had a sense of perception and a perception of sense.

In those days, as now, there were people who were mildly or badly upset by too much talking, too much excitement, too many things going on around them. Sometimes, as today, they recognized the tension, but more often it was subconscious and they felt only the result. Ever since we learned how to make intelligible—I didn't say intelligent!—noises with our vocal chords we have been more or less in a state of tension. In some the very fact that there are other people in the same building creates a desire to talk to them. When that can't be done, a frustration is set up which in turn creates tension and nervousness.

So—the more people we have around us the more tense we are liable to become. You don't have to look far to find examples of this nor do you have to think long to perceive the end result in a world which is becoming more crowded by the day. The history of evolution tells us that those who cannot adjust cannot survive, but I sometimes have nightmares thinking of the race that is liable to evolve if our civilization keeps on its present course.

The tongue and larynx stimulate and are stimulated by the brain. It has been demonstrated many times that children frequently babble themselves into hysterics or nervous breakdowns when they first begin to talk easily. They begin sensibly enough, but end up in a wild medley of words without any reason to them, or else in silly noises. I sometimes wonder if adults are any better or if the whole world is not drifting into a sort of "ducktalk" without any real thought behind it. So many of us have become parrots that the transition to quacks would probably be quite easy.

The cure in these times is the same as it was in medieval days: getting away from the human race for an hour, a day or longer and relaxing in quiet meditation. It worked then and it would work now, but how many of us ever try it? The Quakers understand the value of it; there is much silence at their Sunday meetings and their grace before meat is an unspoken thought. Likewise those Catholics and Protestants who make Retreats realize that it helps both mind and body. And I know it! I am conscious of it from the first plump robinchirp in the grey dawn to the last sweet whistle of the hermit thrush when the mountains are shadowed by the coming night. Sometimes I stop whatever I am doing and just listen to the silence. Sometimes I stand on the knoll between the rows of scarlet strawberries and feast my eyes upon the lovely face of solitude.

Personality Plural

THERE ARE moments when I think that individuality has passed from men to mice. The human beings I know tend more and more to look alike, dress alike, speak alike, act alike and think in identical clichés. But the mice I've met in my rustic mountain home are something else again.

There are, for instance, the mice who insist upon original dying. At night six traps are put out and baited with delicious cheese. The next morning they are untouched, but when I go to get some shoes out of my cupboard I find a mouse in one of them, very dead. (I refuse to discuss here whether said mouse died of asphyxiation or shoeing.)

Perhaps I start to put a bag of flour into a three-foot high metal tin which is always covered. Peering into this food fortress, which I would have declared impregnable to any mouse, I discover a definitely deceased rodent at the bottom of it. No mouse could climb the sheer metal sides of that can. No mouse could jump into it with the top on. No mouse could—but a mouse did. My only theory is that, growing older and less agile or being haunted by fear of a mis-step, he decided to take a quick way out and pay me back for my traps at the same time. He must have jumped to the lid of the tin and then forced himself underneath by a dexterous and determined process which I have no intention of explaining here—much less proving.

I must admit, however, that these otherwise rugged individualists frequently display a talent for revenge which is almost human. In the likewise rugged individuality of my home there are two water pails: one for drinking, one for washing. They have sleek metal sides and sit about three feet from the ground and some eighteen inches away from the wall, on what is known as "the water table." These pails are above the window sill level and so, in the days when I trustingly believed that men were the only originals, I was positive that no mouse could commit suicide in them intentionally or otherwise. So I baited my traps with succulent tidbits and dashed hopefully out of bed in the grisly dawn—to find them untouched to a trap and a mouse in each water pail. This heyday couldn't last, of course. I covered the pails with newspapers—and discovered mouse and paper equally waterlogged by morning. I put boards across—through minute gaps in which several furry strategists managed to wriggle. Now I have fitted metal covers over the pails, but I'm promising nothing.

Needless to say, there are some striking personalities among these redoubtable rodents. I shall not forget the courageous pocket mouse that chewed off part of his foot to get away or that doughty meadow mouse I found glaring at me one morning from behind the kitchen stove, having dragged a trap across two rooms by his tail during the night. In spite of his nocturnal struggles he was ready to do battle again at the flick of a whisker. He was not afraid of me or of death and his fierce eyes told me so in no uncertain terms. What a warrior! Of course I let him go.

But never let it be thought that individuality exists only in the male of the species—particularly in the nesting season, which seems to be all year round. The potential mamas know exactly where I keep my blankets and flannelette sheets, thereby making any resemblance between my storage drawer and a sieve impurely uncoincidental. A nip here, a slash there, a rip-rending time somewhere else and I find my winter or summer clothing and bedding—whichever I happen to need at the moment—completely air-conditioned. My clothes are not safe even when they are practically on me. One winter night I threw a brand new wool dressing-gown over my bed and drew its neck well up around mine. When I woke up one shoulder of that gown had been neatly chewed away. I refused to believe my eyes until I found that a hand would go in one side of the shoulder and out the other with nothing whatsoever to stop it. Thereupon I slammed the bedroom window shut and retreated to the kitchen to get breakfast. Happening to glance out of the kitchen window a little later I beheld an agitated lady mouse, in an interesting condition, running along the bedroom window sill beating frantically at the pane with her tiny front paws. Up and down on her little back legs she teetered, refusing to believe that her lovely new nest wasn't going to be finished in imported brown wool. I found my heart wasn't any more mouseproof than my home. I opened the window, thrust the dressing-gown at her and muttered nobly:

"Here, take it, old girl. You need it more than I do."

But with a frightened squeak Mrs. Mouse ran down the side of the house and disappeared in the snow.

These dapperling dears are also very interested in food matters, judging by the full traps in my root house and the pock-marked look of my more carelessly stored vegetables. My back still remembers the hussy who chewed her way into my potato bin, sinking a joyous tooth at random and forcing me to sort the whole thing over twice in two days. In a bevy of eccentrics she stood out for her consistency. When I mended the first hole she chewed through the mend not once but four times, although it would have been far easier to tackle another spot.

These rodent ructions are all in the past, but Xantippe and Scheherazade are everlastingly present. The former is no true rodent, but it would take an expert to guess it by her actions. According to the textbooks she is a miniature mammal with a fast heart and such a high BMR that she has to eat at least once every hour. This carnivore chit is supposed to live mostly on insects and to be so highly strung that she is liable to die of fright when taken alive. My Xantippe finds it necessary to feed her inch-long frame once a second; she eats anything that is going and is apparently shockproof.

> Little Xantippe lives under a stone,
> Little Xantippe lives all alone.
> Why does she do it? I wish I knew;
> Perhaps it's because Xantippe's a shrew.

Xantippe, as you will remember, was the wife of Socrates and reputed to be a nifty nagger. My Xantippe runs me ragged without emitting more than a squeak of satisfaction when I hurl a boot at her and miss. For three solid weeks she had eluded six traps, eating the cheese (insects, indeed!) from each one and leaving it still set. I even bought a special shrew trap. The only difference is that she doesn't take the cheese from that one. In her luxurious dark fur coat she dashes the few yards from her stone mansion to my humble abode in broad daylight and when she has me helplessly sponge-bathing in the nude she flees furrily over my feet. I have taken to looking out of the window at the nearest hemlock tree and musing on ancient Greece.

> Mousie Scheherazade may be lass or laddie,
> I wouldn't know and I wouldn't care
> For no one can call me faddy.
> All that I know of that little mouse
> That scampers over my little house
> Is that he or she, whichever it be,
> Has done his or her best to entertain me
> With a rooting, scooting, hurry-scurrying,
> Sneaking, squeaking, furry-flurrying
> Not just for a thousand and one mad nights—
> But for eternity!

Scheherazade, that namesake of Persian folklore whom I have glimpsed only by flashlight, has a handsome grey and white fur coat and a heavy foot. Such prancing, such cavorting, such rattling of bric-a-brac and tumbling of shoes. I can hear her setting off my traps one by one on the nights when Xantippe has found better hunting elsewhere. Then there is a run, a long skid over my living-room floor and a bounce into the bedroom. I press my flashlight button. Scheherazade gazes innocently at me from the top of the dressing-table. Beautiful whiskers wave beguilingly:

"Aren't I entertaining you well enough?" they seem to ask with a quiver. "Well, watch me now. I *know* you'll like this!" And my open tin of tooth powder goes over with a crash.

Last night I interrupted a small stranger mouse doing a *pas seul* in my living-room. He didn't run. He simply reared back on his miniature haunches and looked me over. Now what? Perhaps there is something to be said for robots after all.

Spring Cleaning

SPRING HAS swept away the last patch of snow with her green-twigged broom and hung out the clouds to bleach. Housecleaning is in full swing in the bird houses and even human hermits are swept into the rhythm of it. Out go woollens, dust and stale air; in come sunshine, fresh winds and a light-headed, light-bodied feeling that belongs to this month and to no other.

What a fine world it would be if nations could do the same thing! If the old prejudices and fears and obsolete thinking could be heaved out the door to make room for faith and courage and kindness. If even we as individuals could house-clean our hearts as thoroughly as we do our homes and refuse to clutter them up ever again with distrust and anger and misunderstanding.

The beginning of a mountain April is like faith: "the substance of things hoped for, the evidence of things not seen." First there is just a lightening in the sky and a stirring in the blood and the sharp-sweet scent of earth that is being warmed and dried by the sun. The hill streams flash white against deciduous pale green and conifer darkness. The rivers begin to sing their mountain songs and soon they are drunk with the sound of their own wild voices.

I am a little drunk myself, but there is sadness in me also. Everything is so clean and new, so full of hope and promise. It is just as it might have been when man came out of the great ice ages and the spring of earth began. Everything before us—and we have come to this: the shifty eyes of fear, the thin mouth of intolerance, the out-thrust jaw of hatred. We have come to busyness without end and end without meaning.

The words of an old song come into my mind: "Where do we go from here, boys?" They were merry words once. They looked forward to adventure, to new lands and new lives. They were ready to meet victory or defeat with a laugh. But now we say those words slowly, haltingly; feeling that we know only too well where we are going and don't want to think about it. Or we say them restlessly, off the tops of our minds; fearfully determined to still thought with movement. The world has been like a child wilfully tipping over the bowl of its heritage and watching it spill across the table of life without any idea of the value of what it was losing. There would always be more, wouldn't there? Yes—and more people to share it with and less room to eat it in. It was bad enough when we were throwing soil, trees, rivers, animals, fish and birds away so carelessly; it was infinitely worse when we became so earthbound that we felt the only way we could rise was by lightening our ballast of such non-essentials as kindness, courage, self-discipline, independence, the quiet carrying-through and the lilting sense of adventure.

Whatever made us believe that just to be clothed and fed and housed was to be happy? Where do we go from here? I have a gnawing fear sometimes that I know what the answer may be for the world if the human inhabitants of this lovely earth don't realize in time where they are heading and what is sending them there. But when I stand beside my cedar on the knoll with April light spreading across the sky and down the mountains and into the last dark hollow of the forest, I think: this is the way it will come, the knowing and the believing. To waken on a spring morning in my valley is to believe in Heaven.

Pioneering Isn't *That* Easy

DOLLY VARDEN and rainbow trout are jumping in my small river now, while in the pool of the big river steelhead lurk and gleam. Another party of fishermen came in today and I can see the glow of their fire on the little strip of beach just opposite me. Tomorrow is going to be quite a day for the trout and this lone hermit.

In fact, it's going to be quite a summer altogether. More and more people seem to be trying to get away from it all and several of them have decided that what is my Eden could probably be theirs too. A few realize that pioneering is a tough job any way you look at it, but others expect to find security, social and otherwise, with no labour for the rest of their very natural lives.

It isn't that easy. Granted, you *can* live without money if you make your tools of stone, your clothes of cedar bark and eat wild herbs, but such a life would consume an enormous amount of time. Just keeping yourself clothed and fed and housed could use up almost every moment. Your brain would lose its polish because you'd be thinking only far enough to solve the all-important question of whether to go up the mountain after goat or up the river after fish. Contemplation of the spiritual would come out a poor second to lighting the cooking fire without matches or building a shelter without nails.

Even in the greater civilization of my own pioneer life I have to do some tall hustling and wide planning to have enough time for thinking, reading and writing books like this one. For a year after I settled here I had no leisure for such things at all; and I was much younger than many of my correspondents who want not only to pioneer but do something else on the side too. I have never believed that life either began or ended at forty, but there is no doubt that jobs become longer and harder the farther one gets on the shady side of it.

Now suppose we consider that you have decided to throw up your city job and settle across the river from me. You would be starting from scratch: no cleared land, no shelter, no fuel except windfalls. If you don't know anything about the woods, then you're due to learn easy things the hard way, with every muscle and brain cell screeching in protest. But we'll suppose you're not that dumb.

If you intend to build a log cabin—for easier construction, better winter heating, good looks—then you should cut your trees at least half a year before you want to use them. Eight-inch would be your limit on size, I think, and you'll need a pulley to raise the top ones and the ridgepole. Spring is the best time for building as the March snow makes hauling simpler and logs peel most easily in April. As the trees are coming down, a shelter and a woodpile could be going up. You don't have to worry about windbreaks or pure water here, but cedar foundation logs are a must and low ground is a mustn't.

The roof of your house will be of cedar shakes, of course, and if you are wise you'll have tar paper and a course of boards underneath them. These aren't absolutely necessary, but very comfortable and fuel-saving. Oakum and quarter-rounds (wedge-shaped peeled sticks) driven in over the oakum make the best chinking. Clay is good, but will crack from prolonged cabin heat. Moss is a permanent invitation to mice and squirrels. Your floors, like mine, would probably be thick fir shakes and so would outside doors. A heavy job.

Of course there are smooth, beautiful boards of all sorts down in the village. But remember that everything from a match to a sledge hammer has to be packed in on your back across a mountain and through a forest for over three miles. And don't forget that cage and cable. If you don't do some powerful thinking ahead you'll find your building bee in the blind staggers from interruptions for food, tools and that book on "How to Build a Log Cabin and Survive to Live in It."

In fact, I would urge any would-be settler in the wilds to give serious thought to his means of transportation and whether he will be able to cope with it even when he is three score and ten. Not only from the standpoint of energy, but of time. The best plan where I live is to get in a two-year supply of any non-perishables, food or otherwise, and then keep this stock up to par. The division between the store, the garden and the wilderness is settled by the individual's health, wealth and know-how.

The first few months of pioneering are like a three-ring circus. While you're trying to get yourself under cover there's a garden to dig, fish to catch, mice to combat. There's water to carry, wood to cut, campfire cooking and brush-bed sleeping. A woodshed and a you-know-what are necessities, while both wild and tame food will demand a root house. If you can't mend your tools or make them if necessary, then a day or more will be wasted packing new ones in. You'll have to figure out how to pack a stove in too as our winters don't encourage outdoor cooking.

Ah, winter! That's the time to catch your breath and lie long. That's what *you* think. Winter's the time to finish up your buildings, get next year's wood in (a two-year supply is a good idea), make your furniture, throw flats together for your seedlings—and then run panting out to help spring make the ground plantable. From then until the vegetables are stored and the berries bottled there won't be many free moments. When you do find one you'll probably use it for planning a water system and digging over more ground. For one thing's sure: when you begin to live like a pioneer there's no end to it.

Crazy Like a Canoe

I DO SOME crazy things sometimes, but canoeing down either of my swift mountain rivers is the last escapade I'd be liable to embark on. In days gone by, however, more than one person had ideas about the larger stream being navigable.

When I first came here there was the wreck of an old Indian canoe almost in my front yard. The upper rim was of birch bark, the body of white pine. Enough was left to show that it had sharp ends running under water, which placed it as of either Shuswap or Thompson make. Canoes of this type were also in use in Eastern Siberia years ago.

So either this canoe I had found was very old indeed or it had been made by an Indian who believed, wrongly, that such a vessel would be sturdy enough to stand up to the numerous rapids and dangerous currents of this boulder-strewn, tree-filled river. Perhaps it had been made by an Indian for a miner who wanted to get to gold in a hurry. At any rate, it was the type generally used by the Interior tribes because it was light to carry and swift, easy to make and repair. But it damaged and capsized easily.

Certainly this particular canoe had not been made nearby for there is practically no birch near me and not much white pine, although cedar is plentiful. I doubted that it could have come any distance up or down the Teal, so it must have been portaged from the Mallard—over thirty miles—or packed over the mountains. Either thought made me feel very tired. The remains were deep in the gravel of an old bed of the Teal, which tied in with the antiquity theory. I dug them up and packed them out to a neighbour who was over eighty and remembered a lot about such things. The very next night he was burned out and so was my canoe. He couldn't tell me anything anyway.

It was hardly a year later that I found the "dugout"; several miles down the Teal in a part I hadn't explored. It was half-buried in gravel, earth, tree roots and bracken, but intact except for long scars and one great gouge that almost went clean through the spruce wood. I stood and stared at it for a long time, for here was coast work surely; possibly Haida—and how in the name of Ogopogo had a Haida canoe got up in the Cascade mountains? It was a fishing and hunting craft, but the hunting grounds of the Haida are in the Queen Charlotte Islands. It could have held three people easily, but why would even one person be so foolish as to brave this violent mountain river? And why a Haida? In fact, why a canoe? I felt as though I were going around in a tidal whirlpool.

As I dug the canoe out of its leafy bed I thought of the "canoba" I had come across once on a high, forested mesa of the Jemez Mountains of New Mexico. It was a log thirty-five feet long and four feet through at the larger end, hollowed out roughly like a big trough and with the bottom flattened. The nearest Indian pueblo was Santo Domingo, almost twenty miles away, and the canoe lay the same distance from the Rio Grande and the Rio Puerco. The only other water was in mountain streams like these two of mine. There were good piñon pines around, so I could see why the builder might have chosen that spot, but how it could be taken anywhere else and if it ever was I never did discover.

That "canoba" was evidently meant for transport, as the Indians of New Mexico—who are thought to have travelled down through British Columbia after crossing the Bering Strait from Asia—were like the Haidas in making such craft twenty-five to thirty-five feet in length. The Haida canoes made B. G. (before gasboats) were lighter and more graceful than any others on the British Columbia coast. A family craft was capable of carrying up to fifteen people with food, trading goods and baggage. Flat-bottomed, they had an upward curving cutwater bow and a stern that projected backwards besides curving slightly up.

The travelling canoes might be thirty feet longer with a six- to eight-foot beam. A flaring gunwale and long, projecting spurs fore and aft made them very seaworthy. They could carry thirty-five people and up to five tons of freight. The war canoes were about the same length and usually decorated with tribal crests or even human teeth. They had seats, fastened to the sides with cedar roots and supported underneath by a piece of bark carried from bow to stern.

The yellow cedars for them (Sitka spruce was used for smaller, lighter canoes) were felled on a stream bank, roughly trimmed and towed home in summer for winter working. The first shaping was done with adzes and wedges to allow for spreading after the log was hollowed out. By using embers outside and hot water inside—raised to boiling point by red-hot stones—the wood fibres were softened and so a log three feet in diameter could be spread to five feet. It was kept like this by narrow thwarts pegged into the sides. When it had cooled the wood was rigid.

About the long job of smoothing the canoe outside and in I know from working on the one I found, although I didn't make any herring-bone pattern with my adze or use a chisel to lessen water friction. I rubbed with sandpaper instead of sandstone or shark's skin, but the result was much the same. I went higher up the mountains for Sitka spruce and used that with pitch to fill in the gouge. When I finished I was as proud as though I had done the whole thing from scratch and my crest was a killer whale instead of a crabbed hermit.

A fine canoe like that should go places. So we went. I launched her on a July day when the water was medium-high and medium-quiet. For half a mile, for a mile my red cedar paddle kept us in midstream and I shouted with joy because the canoe was living and so was I. We went faster and faster. Canyon walls grew up around us—and suddenly I was in icy water grabbing for a rock-jammed log which luckily was there. I never saw the canoe again, although I searched many times. Climbing out of that canyon was the worst job I ever tackled.

I said that canoeing down either of my rivers was the last escapade I'd be liable to embark on. It almost was.

Strangers of the Earth

IN THE LONG summer evenings, when my day's work is over, I sometimes go up to the knoll under the big cedar and watch darkness climb the mountains from the evergreen forests of my valley. The rivers murmur companionably, Maestro begins his usual twilight song, and the night wind which blows across my garden carries the very scent of home.

Everything is familiar and dear and once again I feel that rush of joyous thankfulness that I have been given so much of beauty, so much of peace, so much of friendship. For a little while I can forget the strangeness of the outside world and the strangers who inhabit it.

We are all strangers here, but no one more so than the person who is out of step with the time. If you are that person you will be understood—and then only imperfectly—by just one or two of all those you know and perhaps by none at all. To the others you will always be suspect. The timid will be afraid to be seen with you; the bold will say they cannot be bothered with anyone who is more interested in the future of the world than in whether today's market is going up or the price of tomorrow's whisky going down.

Most of this ostracism will bother you very little for there is nothing you like better than quietness and privacy. But not every moment of your life. In books you can find the comradeship and understanding you are denied by living men, but even so you are hungry for a good heart-to-heart talk with someone who comprehends you intellectually and emotionally. If you are lucky you will come across one or two people with whom you can exchange ideas, and if you are luckier still you will marry one of them.

But you are still The Stranger. In the glibness of social intercourse you are left floundering because you know that time is going and you want so desperately to say something worth while before it is gone. Yet neither to your mate nor to your friends can you speak that inmost word, convey that inmost thought which so longs to be spoken and heard and understood. And time is slipping by.

That urgent sense of the shortness of life, perhaps more than anything else, distinguishes the man out of step with his time from his fellow beings. He sees time wasting everywhere around him and he is disgusted and alarmed. He knows that it is all wrong; that life is precious and should be used for precious things. Not that he believes in all work and no play, but simply that his idea of play differs from the bridging, gossiping, clock-watching, pulp-reading average. To him play is a change of occupation—perhaps from writing to splitting wood—while relaxation is letting go completely in sleep, laughter or lying on a summer hill watching the clouds drift over and "growing soul."

He looks down on the "kingdoms of the world" from that height, seeing them not only as they are but as they should be. He feels closer to the simplicity and beauty of nature than to the monstrosities erected by man, and closeness to earth and sky and tree brings a deep joy welling up inside him. These are the eternal verities and he feels brotherhood with them because he has assessed the value of that which is eternal in himself.

If the man out of step with his time becomes famous, then all is forgiven. It won't matter how eccentric he has seemed or the muddle he has made of his life judged by the social yardstick. But unfortunately, this doesn't happen very often, for The Stranger is usually not only out of step with his time but ahead of it, and so becomes The Friend only after he is dead. Then the people heap flowers on his grave and conveniently forget that their fathers crucified him. Failing the hope of this posthumous chaplet of bay, he has only one recourse: to build such strength within himself that nothing outside can hurt or sway him. To know that, for himself, he is right and that this feeling of rightness is the only thing that really matters.

Wilderness Love Story

"WELL," exclaimed a strange female voice behind me, "so you *do* live in a house!"

That's the trouble with a winter that has less snow than usual. The rivers get fordable early and you never know all summer when you are going to look up and find a strange face leering at you. Not that this particular stranger leered; she couldn't very well with her mouth wide open in astonishment. She just kept looking from me to the house and back to me again as though she thought I ought to be wearing a leopard skin and living in trees.

Actually I had on about as little: shorts and top. I've slept in trees too, in snake country. But I could see the lady was disappointed and I didn't know how to make it up to her. I looked up on the big woodpile at the edge of the forest to see if Grandfather Cougar was taking an afternoon nap there. Not a sign of the good-for-nothing fellow. I listened for crashings in the underbrush which would mean that some of my black bear chums had outreached themselves on the salmonberries. Then I thought of a sure-fire hit and started whistling in a come-hither manner which slightly disconcerted my guest. In a moment she was more than slightly anything. Out from the woodshed marched Mrs. Skunk and her six babies and came towards us in single file. The lady skirled like a bagpipe and then I heard my front door bang and saw the cabin shake as she bounded across the living-room floor, trying to get as far away as possible. I went into the kitchen to get milk for my black and white performers—who had never done the trick so well before in spite of weeks of whistling patience on my part. Then I put the kettle on to boil for some nerve-settling Labrador tea.

Over the tea I found out that Miss Linton—as we'll call her, because it isn't her name—had read some of my pieces in *The Vancouver Sun* and then heard my name when she was visiting in the village. So she'd come looking for me through the woods and over the river and here I was, not wild at all but only slightly pixilated. I don't know just what she thought of me after we'd eaten hot biscuits with black currant jam and talked about Marcel Proust, whose books she spotted on my shelves. She kept looking nervously around until we were on the cage and I heard her sigh relievedly when she had negotiated the platform ladder on the other side and stood on firm ground once more. I swore her to secrecy as to my whereabouts and we parted good friends in spite of the black and white parade. I was glad she hadn't come in the evening when there might have been a bobcat peering in the window or my big coyote pal sneaking up for a handout.

But after she had gone and I was back digging over ground for more lettuce and peas, I began to think about what she had said concerning living in a house. She hadn't been far off about the way I felt about it. I had always disliked houses, without actually knowing that I did. I remember the tree-rooms I had as a child: in shrubbery, in a patch of wood, anywhere that I could draw branches close around me and shut out brick and steel. When I was older I used to take jam-packed humid streetcars out to the city limits and then walk miles to find what could pass as a wood. Preferably one with a glade where I could sit and imagine that I was in a greenhouse built of earth and sky.

I don't know just what it was about houses that made me so uncomfortable. It wasn't just the love of the outdoors, although that was part of it. It was a definite feeling that when a door closed behind me I was separated from something which was vital to the health of mind and body. I had a lonely feeling, as though I had left friends behind. I had a hungry feeling, as though something way down deep inside me had been cut off from nourishment. I didn't put it into words; I hardly put it into thoughts. It was simply there and the only time it lessened was when I could stand in a vacant city lot looking up at the stars or steal hours from rest to sit on the waterfront in summer dawn with the town slumbering behind me. Yet even on the rare country Sundays I never lost the feeling entirely. You see, I always had to come back again.

But one day I didn't come back. I kept right on going until I was in the Cascade Mountains. I found a shack and made it into a home. So there I was—in another house. Yet it wasn't the same at all. It never has been; not from the first moment. In fact, I have never been quite sure that my little cabin didn't spring originally from the ground, like the tall trees which grow around it. Perhaps with green thought for seed and the free wind to carry it to my valley. It feels rooted in the peaceful earth and when I stand across the Teal to look at it the picture is satisfyingly complete. Not a jarring note, nothing out of place, not a thing there that shouldn't be.

Oh, yes, I know all the modern tabus on "sentimental nature writing," on assuming that animals can talk in their own way and that plants react to people. Maybe it is all silly sentiment. I don't know. But I do know that persons react to places, just as they do to other people. According to their sensitivity, they react sharply or sluggishly to what in a human being would be called personality. Certainly it has always been that way with me. I have been in places I liked at first glimpse, places I distrusted, places I wanted to leave as quickly as possible. Always in the back of my mind was the desire for that one perfect place where I could feel fulfilled and truly at home.

I found it. I knew I had the moment I entered the mountain-fenced valley and saw the silvery shake roof of a cabin trying to peer at me over fireweed and salmonberry brush. I have known it all through the years since and I can't imagine not knowing it forever. The shakes are dark red this season and the cabin has changed in many ways, both inside and out. But whenever I want to add something that isn't right, I know it. Just as I know when I want to do something that is wrong for me, however right it might be for someone else.

So my cabin is simple—as I try to be. Books, a few fitting ornaments, just the tools and furnishings that are needed to carry on uncomplicated living—and nearly all of them homemade. Everything fits. It is all where it should be. When I go in at the big fir door it is as though I were pushing back a tree branch to enter one of the glades of my childhood. There is no sense of being closed in or shut away. When I fling out of the house into the first breath of morning I am simply moving from one glade to a larger, more open one. Everywhere there is warmth and kindliness, humour and courage, freedom and content. That is the way it should be when you come home.

It reads like a love story, doesn't it? I suppose it is—and like all great loves it has a great price. Part of it I have told you already; that had to do with the past and the present. The other is tied to the future and it's harder to phrase. I suppose it is simply this: that if ever I insist upon putting something or someone into my cabin that doesn't belong there, then I shall lose my home. And if ever that time comes—I can't imagine it!—when I have learned all my valley can teach me and should move on to learn more, then in some way or other I shall be driven out. I would never go willingly. But the greater the love the greater may have to be the sacrifice.

So the lady was right after all: I should be living in a tree and in a way I am. But Grandfather Cougar would never give me that sleek, tawny coat of his to wear.

Insurance for Living

MANY PEOPLE have said to me: "But your valley in the Cascades can't possibly be as wonderful as you say it is." Well, that depends on what sort of person you are. To the confirmed city lover it would be a lonely, fearsome place full of claustrophobic mountains and wild beasts, hard living and no plumbing. To the farmer it would seem crammed with stumps to break his plough, with bushes and trees that were stealing moisture from the soil, with obstreperous rivers that thought little of bridges. He would be exasperated with the whole thing in no time. Certainly the average woman wouldn't like my valley. What, no neighbours to gossip with, no electrical whoozits—not to mention noises in the night that could be *anything*!

I can just hear all these good people: "It's so dark! It's so isolated! You have to work so hard! Think of all those cougars and bears wandering around!" Granted. It *is* dark—in the rainy days of fall when the sun has vanished behind the mountains and the snows have not yet come. It *is* isolated— thank heaven, and may it always be that way! I *do* have to work hard—and I'm a better person physically and mentally for that. There *are* a lot of bears and cougars—but they're the finest neighbours I know; they don't gossip or quarrel and, so far, they have interfered in no way whatsoever with my life, liberty, pursuit of happiness and food. They eat berries and roots outside my valley, yes. Roots and berries on my property, no. Don't ask me why. I've been trying to solve that riddle for a long time. If this were a hundred years ago I would probably be accused of witchcraft, for my nearest neighbours are so plagued by the depredations of animals and birds that only two of them are still trying to have a garden.

Is my valley beautiful? So far only confirmed mountain-haters have failed to agree that it is. Of course if you insist on your land lying down flat or your hills being brown, then my tall peaks with their forests of evergreen might seem bizarre and ugly to you. I'm being reasonable about this, you understand, although it is all I can do to keep from shouting: "How *can* you feel that way? How can you possibly not rave yourself hoarse over my mountains crowned with snow, my singing rivers, the bird song of my forest almost primeval?" I have dreamed of such beauty all my life and I have sought it everywhere, but this is the only place I have found it in true perfection. But that, you will say, is being sentimental and silly; now let's be practical. You can't eat scenery, can you?

No, but you can eat deer and mountain goat, bear steaks and grouse meat, and they are all around you in these same mountains. You can eat fish—and my two rivers are full of steelhead, Dolly Varden and brook trout. If you prefer lake angling there are alpine gems set in wildflowers where high altitude fins flash freely. You can eat sixteen varieties of berries—each and every one of them growing wild in my valley or on the hills around. There are wild roots and shoots galore; enough to fulfil every requirement for vitamins and minerals—and even give you that overstuffed feeling, if you insist on it.

Are you thirsty? The water in my smaller river has perfect purity for I am the only person living on it from its source in two mountain springs to where it empties into the larger Teal at my front door. Something stronger than that? Well, have you ever tried dandelion wine, elderberry wine, blackberry cordial, cherry bounce? Ah! Now, how about a cigarette of kinnikinnick—if you must smoke—and perhaps you would like to wash your hands with wild syringa soap or some made from bear grass bulbs?

The check? There isn't one. Everything I have mentioned is yours for the taking, either in my valley or on its guardian mountains, although I admit you would have to know a little botany to find some of the foods. But there is a price on this meal, as there is on everything else in the world. The best things in life are *not* free; we merely pay for them in different media of exchange. The price is too high? I'm sorry, for I believe it is part of the price we shall all have to pay some day in order to retain the liberty and happiness of our way of life.

That brings us to the things which we cannot touch or smell or taste, but which are no more divided from the practical than body and soul are disunited. There is the satisfaction of living each day to its fullest and receiving from each night's sleep the vitality of deep content. No one knows morning who has not seen the dawn. No, more than that: who has not seen the summer world in that grey cocoon of silence which precedes the sunrise. What a sense of adventure there is in being out at this hour when all other life seems sleeping! I only wish I could describe that leap of the heart which comes each time I walk out my door into this anteroom of light which divides night from day.

In spring I do my planting at this time and continue it while the clouds over Evergreen Mountain change from grey to ivory to pale rose to flamingo and the blue of the sky deepens and deepens until you would swear that all the seas had been drowned in it. What experiences I have shared with hill and heaven and water and rich earth! Could anyone be luckier than I?

The day passes as it has begun: in hard work done for the love of it. There is never an hour without something ahead to accomplish which will call out every bit of ingenuity I possess. That is the way of pioneer living. Things are not done for you; you do them yourself and you put the best of yourself into them. Your children make their own fun and their own toys. They are not spectators of life; they are right in the middle of it. When they grow up they won't give you a "thank you" for parental politics or hamstringing handouts.

Your insurance against sickness is healthy living, carefulness and the medicines which are all around you in the woods and clearings. Have you eaten too much of the good fare of the mountains? Here are the roots of Oregon grape or ginger to relieve you or, if you have guzzled too many salmonberries, you should try a hair of the dog that bit you: a tea of salmonberry bark. Have you cut yourself on sword fern or stabbed a devil's club thorn into your hand? Put a yarrow or heal-all plaster on it at once. If it is bleeding badly the pitch of Balsam fir will help it or soothe the bad bruise you got chasing that mountain goat for supper. The inner bark of the poplar will provide an efficient laxative or you can obtain one from the cascara bush, dogbane roots or milkweed plant. However, you won't have much use for anything like that in this active life. If too much activity is unnerving, the roots of the dwarf dogwood should calm you. The wilderness teas—fireweed, ginger, sage, white birch or black alder will help to keep you in good condition. Dwarf dogwood for malaria, heal-all for quinsy, onions for croup, burdock for bad blood, Solomon's seal for rheumatism, juniper tea for kidney trouble, wild cherry bark mixture for that bad cough—here they all are in Nature's medicine chest.

Your unemployment insurance is a full woodshed and a root house stocked with meat, fish, game and fruit of your own canning or smoking; with vegetables stored in boxes or hanging from the roof. Crocks of sauerkraut and dills stand on the floor with gallon bottles of rose hip and blue elderberry syrup. Lift the box covers and you will find potatoes, carrots, beets, turnips and kohl rabi from the garden. Cabbages, cauliflowers, brussels sprouts, broccoli and, if it is early winter, tomatoes will dangle over your head. In the attics of the house the onions are stored and the herbs are drying.

In the wilderness we prepare in the grand manner for the siege of winter and at no season of the year does my house lack provender enough to see me through any bad turn of fortune. There is nothing I need buy if the trails are blocked with snow, if money is lacking or an unavoidable accident has confined me to the house. Of course there will be dripping for butter, sugar beet syrup or roots of the edible thistle for sweetness—but what of that? If I am unable to bake my sourdough bread, potatoes will take its place. If it were not for the big drum of powdered milk in my cellar, the eggs I have candled and the hundred pound sack of rolled oats in my kitchen perhaps my diet would seem monotonous by modern standards—but surely nourishing.

As for my old age pension, I shall begin to collect it at the usual time, but not in the usual form. I shall know when it arrives by the fact that, although I have to slow down a bit and cut my garden chores a mite, I can still shoulder a pack with the other oldsters of these mountains and provide far more for myself than I need. I shall know it by my clear, bright eyes when those of my city friends are rheumy and sad; by my spare, hardy body and fit mind when those of my urban acquaintances are fat or filled with disease. Most of all I shall know it by the way my heart still leaps to meet the day and adventures into the wonderment of night. When, one crisp autumn morning perhaps, I see my last trail opening up ahead of me I shall follow it through the fire of the earth I love. I shall follow it up my dear mountains and, finally, over that one mountain too many. When the last darkness comes, it, too, will be adventure.

Cabin Bogey Man

It is in November that the moon the Indians call the Ice Moon sails high above Cougar and floods my valley with light. The sight of it is more welcome now than at any other time of year. There is no sunlight in the days and it is only the seeking eye which can find colours other than the browns, greys and greens of forest, mountain and river. But on moonlight nights there are rainbows everywhere as the moonbeams strike colour from grass and bush and tree. Boulders are jewelled platinum against onyx water and the smoke from my chimney is like an old, rich tapestry of faded hues unrolling upon the counter of the night.

Let no one believe that November is not exciting. There is every variety of weather in it; more than in any other month except March. There are days when the temperature hovers around sixty and the air is mild as milk. There are nights when I go to bed with wood winds and drums rendering The Storm and wake up to the white silence of snow. Sometimes mist, incensed with wet leaves and earth, drifts across my valley as my mountains take the veil. Such a soft graceful thing, mist; transmuted to rare beauty by the sun and moon. It resembles a quiet, gracious personality which needs the sun of a great love or the moon of a great heroism to bring out its inner grandeur.

There are nights and days when my valley is filled with the clamour of rivers; those great brown bullies filled with importance—and rain. The morning hours are bright with the sun which still shines across the Teal and on all the mountain tops. The afternoons are chilly and dark in my clearing, heavy with the moisture that will drip from every blade and branch until frost turns it into white cellophane. But when that first frost comes, then my valley is fairyland indeed. It glitters and sparkles and glints and as the cold continues the frost crystals get bigger and brighter. Branches of infant evergreens droop white plumes and even the gravelled walks have a rimed shimmer. Wood splits easily and other chores seem lighter because of the lift which comes from dryer, cleaner air.

Gradually the pendulum of the weather swings more steadily towards winter. When the mist curtains part, the snow-covered backdrop of Evergreen appears and Fireweed is white from crown almost to base. The rivers become more and more sedate and it is difficult to realize that they could have thrown such tantrums just a short while ago. My valley is a symphony of green and white, for the frost has not yet been able to wither the grass, ferns and remaining alder leaves. Rain changes to hail and then to snow. First the flakes are grey and splashy; then they become big and fluffy and very white. Gradually they take on the consistency of sugar and then, as the mercury continues to drop, of salt. I rescue the last greens from the garden and get out the snow shovel. Winter has arrived and there is no guest more welcome in my house.

But the winter of a mountain November is not always a quiet, well-behaved visitor. Sometimes I waken at night to hear the wild song of the conifers as they sway in their ancient storm dance. Snow spume scuds across the clearing to break on the bark walls of my cabin. The little house trembles and I, lying warm and snug in my cedar bunk, think what a wild night it must be outside. Yet when I go out to share in this midnight madness I find that the sounds which had come funnelled down to my bed with so much intensity now flow wide and high above me. Only the tops of the evergreens are writhing and their song seems far away and long ago. Snow spatters here and there under a gust of wind, but the rivers flow silently and my valley seems little disturbed by all the uproar of high places. "Not a wild night at all," I think as I turn to go in. Yet as soon as I have closed the door I would swear that all the furies were holding carnival outside.

This is a strange thing and one which I cannot describe adequately. I have noticed it at other seasons. Sometimes when the alarm clock goes off in the middle of the night to waken me for my pre- or post-hibernation visit to town I hear rain slashing down on my shake roof and the wind rushing around in the darkness outside. I think crossly, "It would be like this just when I don't want to be bothered with my bone drys!" and have visions of a trail strewn with windfalls. Then I open the door and stand on the side porch. Where is all this night of drenching terror? Only the rivers seem to know anything about it and it is natural enough that they should be shouting at this time of year. There is rain, but it is falling lightly and softly. The wind is so busy rattling the door of Heaven that I know it isn't even going to be present on the forest trails. It is a nice night to walk over Fireweed to the little branch railroad and my city top coat will be just the thing to wear.

Perhaps it's the same with our troubles. If we lie in bed and listen to them blowing and snorting in the darkness, our imagination is liable to take the bit in its teeth and conjure up all sorts of dreadful future happenings. Everything seems so much worse when we cower away from it, inactive and afraid. But if we get up and fling the doors of our minds wide open, if we step out boldly into the night, ready to come to grips with whatever it holds, we find that there is very little to worry about after all. It may be a wind that is so far away that we shouldn't be concerning ourselves with it; or a gentle rain that, at the very worst, is only going to give us a bit of a wetting. Even if the storm *is* actually raging around our doors—which only happens once or twice in a lifetime and sometimes never, though a lot of people won't believe me!—if we go out to grapple with it we shall be so busy that before we know it the whole thing has blown over and the homestead of our life is quiet once again.

When I waken to wind or sleet or snow in the November night I know that what I am hearing inside my cabin is magnified and unreal. Outside there is only a little preliminary and stubborn tossing going on before my valley settles down into the white sleep of December.

Wilderness Wayfarers

WHERE I live, travel is strictly by shank's mare, although it is possible to take a pack horse over some of the trails. But not to ride the horse yourself. It would only be a matter of time before it would walk away from under you as you dangled on a tree branch. So we don't get many visitors and those who do come usually fall into those categories which wilderness dwellers have always known: prospectors, timber cruisers, fishermen and hunters. The ones who can't be catalogued in this way usually have a purpose which, good or bad, is never a secret from us for long. Certainly this would be the worst place in the world for a law breaker to hide out, for our grapevine outdoes the tom-tom and all strangers must stand and deliver an account of themselves.

Each summer there is an influx of would-be placer miners who have taken the School of Mines course in Vancouver during the winter and now are all set to make their fortune. Some walk in with big ill-balanced packs on their backs, take over a deserted cabin and operate on the proverbial shoestring. They make sluiceboxes of cedar shakes, shovel gravel ten hours a day and work themselves thin crowbarring the huge river boulders. To be strictly honest, I have seen just four groups in seven years who worked that hard. The rest of the "pack rat" fraternity, as we call them, usually pull up stakes pretty soon or settle down to a lazy summer of living off the country. That is the derivation of the name they go by—and which most of us here have gone by before we settled down. It is not as uncomplimentary as it sounds, but simply denotes someone who picks up anything around the country to which no one seems to have a claim. The animal pack rat is quite a decent rodent that always "pays" for its plunder.

Other prospectors, who have hopes of raising capital, come in with big ideas of dredging the rivers and becoming millionaires in no time. These are people who have little or no acquaintance with the aforementioned boulders or with the flash floods which can raise the height of our mountain streams four feet in an hour. Some of them seem amazingly impractical in other ways also. A group of three came in—and speedily went out again—in October, which is the month our hard frosts begin.

"Now," declared one of our sourdough prospectors, "I can throw away my glasses. I've seen everything. I've seen three placer miners arrive just before winter in a strange place with nothing in their packs but food and expect the folks around to supply them with everything else—including a house to keep it in."

The next September two men arrived who said they had filed on the land just across the river from me, but who didn't seem to be doing much about it. One day, going over the mountain to visit a neighbour, I found three small boxes addressed to me lying at the head of my trail. I thought one of my neighbours had very kindly packed them in for me, but on my way home that evening I ran into one of the newly-arrived placer miners who informed me that he had taken them there and later picked them up and carried them down to the river as he was going that way.

"But," said this husky-looking chap in his thirties, "I didn't dare wade across that river with a load like that. If I had slipped it would have been good-bye in that current. I waded over myself and left a note on your porch, but not with that load—no, sirree! What a place you live in! I'd be scared to death to stay out there alone."

Ah, these great, brave he-men who come out to subdue the wilderness bare-handed! I might mention that the parcels weighed about thirty pounds and that when I came back I had another thirty or so to add to them—but I waded the river with a pack on my back and both hands full. The current is strong—more than one person has been drowned in that stream when it was roaring—but when the water is low it can't push you around very much. I wade whenever I can for it is much easier than pulling myself over by the cage and cable which is my only other means of crossing the river.

Placer miners come and placer miners go, but our streams flow on forever. They have seen hundreds of gold miners since 1859 and the good colours they showed once have disappeared long ago. But each year the gold-fevered hopefuls arrive and each year we fill them with food and tall tales of the tall timber. No one can do the latter quite as well as an old prospector!

The timber cruisers have not much better luck. The district has been logged off pretty stringently in the most accessible parts and to get logs out of the other districts would take a young fortune. Occasionally a small pole-cutting outfit comes in—leaving the woods a shambles, in spite of the British Columbia law that all slashings must be cleaned up. Now there is talk of a big company bringing in "cats," pushing roads through and tearing the heartwood out of our wilderness. Maybe it's true this time. Meanwhile we pick the timber cruisers' brains over cups of tea and regale them with the anecdotes the prospectors might not have swallowed.

The fishermen and hunters provide our main topics of conversation during the long winter. Those who come up here every season are on a special footing, but we show the others no mercy. To our way of thinking a "dude" may do anything. Some of them really fish hard—and the fishing is good—but in a number of cases their equipment consists of 5% fishing tackle and 95% beer. When I hear loud yells at the big pool across the river from me, I can usually figure that the fish will be a lot less disturbed than I for the next few nights and days. Once a party of "sportsmen" dynamited this pool and left the shores littered with dead and dying trout. That and stealing a man's food cache are two things we wilderness dwellers do not forgive. But we are generally glad to yarn with any of these holiday makers—how else would we lay in our winter supply of talk?—and it is nice to be able to tell someone the stories that even the prospectors and timber cruisers wouldn't believe.

Fortunately for our safety the hunting is pretty poor in this district. Cougars and coyotes are fairly plentiful and have either killed or run off the deer. The mountain goats are too wary and wise to be taken without a lot of trouble, while the ducks never come in flocks nor the grouse in any great numbers. Sometimes we wonder if, in desperation, the hunters have decided to stalk the natives in lieu of better game. One autumn I was digging over new ground on my lower flat when a bullet splintered a rock not two feet away from me. I dived behind a big cedar stump not a moment too soon. The next shot hit the shovel I had thrown down!

"Oh, yes," admitted this sportsman when I had halted his fusilade with shouts and crossed the river to give him a piece of my mind, "I saw your house, but it didn't look as though anyone were around and I wanted to try my gun out. It hasn't been shooting well lately."

Even a whole red uniform wouldn't be proof against such a trigger-happy mind.

Other travellers think I am the local ferryman and shout imperiously to be taken over on my cage—in spite of the large "Private Property" sign I have had to put up near the river. One man wandered up onto the cage platform and began to haul away at the pulley ropes which I have attached beside the cable so guests can pull the cage over to the other side themselves. Finally he took them out of the pulley altogether and threw them in the river! I had been part way up the mountain behind my cabin when I saw him. When I finally got down he had disappeared and I spent a jolly two hours disentangling my rope and getting it in working order again.

Another day two men wanted to come over, so I unhooked the cage at my side of the river and signalled them to pull it towards them by the pulley rope. They seemed to have a bad time getting it there and an even worse time holding it so they could both get on. I could see that one man distrusted the whole matter thoroughly. After fifteen minutes or so they gave up the struggle and went away and I hauled the cage in again. They told someone later that "it's as much as your life is worth to go across on that contraption."

Contraption or no it is all I've got and I like it. Swinging out over space on two boards slung on a steel rope anchored to two big firs at either end makes me feel like a real pioneer. I've been using it for years in lieu of the bridge which isn't there— or anywhere for thirty miles in one direction and double that in the other. It gives some women screaming hysterics and I'll admit that it's a novel sensation. In warm weather the cable sags and the pulling is hard. In rain it is slippery and in winter so slick with frost that it is all I can do to get myself over at all. But it's a better protection against unwanted visitors than a bridge ever could be.

In the old days explorers and prospectors would fall a big tree across a river that wasn't fordable. When the big trees gave out the wilderness wayfarer would string a cable over a stream and some of these still remain in out of the way places. Mine has been in use nearly fifty years and I believe my neighbours are now making bets on (a) when either or both of the anchor trees will fall and (b) when the cable will snap as I am pulling across and that be the end of both of us. Meanwhile I grease that cable once a year, haul over on it once a month for mail and supplies and enjoy the horrified expressions of those visitors who have forgotten or never knew the bright face of adventure.

December Garden

DECEMBER is the Moon of the Frozen Mist when quietness comes to the forest and my small river goes into its half sleep. The voice of the big river drops lower and lower from its shouting of November while snow falls softly in the lamplight. When I go out into the candid, unmarked world of morning I feel as though I should tiptoe and be hushed because of all this winter beauty.

Strangely enough, it makes me think of a garden; not just any garden, but of that first Garden, Eden. It is always depicted as having eternal summer—as indeed it might if it was in Mesopotamia, as some archaeologists say—but to me it has winter also: a winter like my valley when it is covered with the frozen mist from heaven and flowers bloom on my windowpane.

Those flowers are blue and white and a strange elusive red in the December moonlight when I get up in the mornings now. They resemble spears of grass, twigs and branches, miniature conifers, tiny ferns, petals and whole blooms. When I look at them under a magnifying glass I feel as though I were in some alpine meadow in the first dawn of the world.

Sometimes I make these bouquets grow by holding a lighted candle to a window covered with a heavy film of granular frost. This thins and becomes watery under the heat. When I take my candle away new designs begin to form where the glass is wet; the variety of moisture and temperature, cleanliness and dustiness in various spots helping to make each pattern different from another. At other times I merely blow my warm breath against the frosted pane to have new blossoms in my "window-box."

Outside there are snowflake flowers, made of dust and water—as are we ourselves. They are always white here unless fir pollen changes them to pale daffodil. But in Baffin Land they might be green, in southern Europe red, because of coloured vegetable organisms growing among them. Even in summer I know that these crystals may be found in the highest clouds over my mountains, while now they are in every cloud that sails far above tall Ipo or grazes the top of lower Evergreen.

The higher they are, the smaller in size, but all of them are usually six-sided with their delicate filaments at an angle of 60 degrees or a multiple of that number. Each crystal is absolutely symmetrical, with all angles equal. But shape and texture, as well as size, depend upon the humidity and temperature of the air. I find that when the stars spark in my mountain sky and the air is crisp as good thought that the snowflowers are brighter, although less intricate and lovely, than those of warmer times. No two are ever alike—as Wilson Bentley, the American naturalist, discovered after he had spent forty years photographing them.

"How full of creative genius is the air in which these flowers are generated!" exclaimed Thoreau. "I should hardly admire them more if real stars fell and lodged on my coat. Nature is full of genius, full of divinity. Nothing is cheap or coarse, neither dewdrops nor snowflakes. And as surely as the petals of a flower are fixed, each of these countless snow-stars come whirling to earth, pronouncing thus, with emphasis, the number six."

The words "flake" and "flock" both derive from the Latin word *floccus*, meaning "a lock of wool." So generally the crystals in any one storm are the same shape and type, just as are the sheep of any one flock. As white as the wool of any lamb, one snowflake seems insignificant; but millions together can paralyse a great city, just as a flock of sheep on the tracks can halt a swift express train.

"Hast thou entered into the treasures of the snow?" asks Job. I feel that I have when I dig deep into what seems like sapphires. But on my shovel I find that I have diamonds only and that the snow-blue light—like all true beauty and happiness—can never be grasped in the hand or held for dissection.

Cutting, in March, through the pile of snow with which I bank my cabin I find dry layers which fell in zero mid-winter and the more humid layers of late autumn and early spring; almost like the wet and dry seasonal rings of a tree. The latter make a good foundation for my "insulation" and also melt rapidly so the sun can get at the harder flakes below. They protect the bulbs and roots in the ground from freezing and then run off into the soil to help the flowers of summer grow. At the edge of my rivers are granular snow crystals which melt into the waters to preserve and beautify the land.

Where there are flowers there must be buds also. I find them brown and red on the vine and broadleaf maples, silver on the willow, gummy safron on the cottonwood, hard yellow-brown on the elder. Each one is wrapped in a waterproof mackinaw of minute scales and sits on its twig in such a position as to get the maximum of sunlight when that golden gardener first tops the height of Evergreen again.

The trunks of alders are argent against the snow and a few dried leaves still cling to their branches. The stems of western dogwood are scarlet and its berries winter-white. The red elderberry has a little wizened fruit on which the black and azure stellar jay will make a last feast. On the apple trees, in sheltered rockeries and a nook of strawberry bed, frosted leaves—red, yellow, brown and even green—look like sugar plums hidden by fairies. Cedar and fir and hemlock seem greener than ever and from them the snow falls in masses with a plopping noise, making hoof-print patterns on the ground below.

There are other prints also—for what would Eden be without animals and birds? Soon it will be time to decorate the Bird's Christmas Tree, a lovely young balsam growing not far from my front door. There will be bones with bits of meat still on them, doughnuts hung from branches by wires and suet wound round and round with red string, swinging gaily in the sparkling wind. There will be bacon rind or salt pork too and "yule logs": very small logs bored with holes into which I push seeds in grease, seeds in peanut butter or anything I think the bird family would like. More seeds will be sprinkled on the snow under every tree on the knoll or at the edge of the forest.

To every child the world is a garden and each morning is the first morning of the earth. All is enchantment and an aching wonder. How marvellous the smell of earth and roses, the dance of a butterfly, the spiralling of a leaf! How exciting to race the wind, to walk face upward in the rain, to try to catch wild snowflakes in a mittened hand! But how fragile and brief this wonder before the onslaught of the world. Soon the weather will be grumbling and the flowers spreading hay fever; fallen leaves and fallen snow mean only work and worry.

I am glad for many things, but gladdest of all because my heart still leaps when the first snowfall comes or I find the first flower of spring. It drums with exultation when the wild geese cry over or the wind strides roaring across my valley. It is hushed and quiet in a winter dawn when even a hurried heartbeat might disturb the feathery balance of new snow.

Every morning is a new day, the first day of the world for me. I shall be praying when I watch the rosy clouds glowing over Fireweed and the sky change from midnight blue to azure. I shall be hymning all day as I glory in bud and frost flower, silver-framed river and silver-crowned mountains. What prayer could I say that would be more than bringing a hurt chickadee in out of the cold? What hymn could be more joyful than standing in happiness too great for words, knee-deep in snow and moonlight? For this is the child's heart and this is truly love.

Merry Christmas To All

ALL DAY the snow had been coming down; big white flakes that seemed to be falling of their own weight, though they were really as light as the thistledown they covered in my clearing. All day the music of the rivers had been fading, until now it was only a thread of sound—or was it memory? All day the high mountains surrounding my valley had been softly receding. Then they disappeared entirely and opal filled the air where they had been.

It was evening and in the mellow light from my living-room oil lamp the six-sided space ships came softly, unhurriedly to earth in their tens of trillions. The paths to the rivers, shovelled that morning, were buried again in crystals and beyond them the uncleared trails had become one with drift and rise and hollow. On the fire-scarred mountain I must climb to reach the nearest house four miles away, the snow would be waist deep by now. Too deep for me, loaded with a packsack of gifts and city clothes. This was not ski country and my bearpaw snowshoes had been loaned and lost.

Two days before Christmas and my plans in tatters? Plans to get up at 3 a.m. and walk over the mountain to connect with a speeder leaving at six for the nearest railroad station. (The branch line had been closed down since the first snowfall in October.) There I was to catch a train for city celebrations in the home of friends. Now I would do none of this at all but spend Christmas, New Year's and probably the rest of the winter snowed in with solitude.

For a few moments I thought regretfully of baths and lights and of warmth which I didn't have to axe into existence; of that glorious promised turkey and the sparkling shop windows. Most of all I thought of good talk and good friends. The door to all this had been slammed shut in my face and as I unpacked the rucksack I would have carried to town I took out a few bright expectations too. But I have always believed that when one door closes another opens. So a door had opened now for me. Where was it and what was behind it?

Having forgotten to reset the time clock in my mind, I woke up promptly at 3 a.m. The cabin, flake insulated, was hardly cold though the temperature must have been in its teens. Snowlight and fading moonlight—(the moon had gone down behind the mountains)—gave my bedroom a Regal lily shining. White, blue and pale cerise frost flowers bloomed on every windowpane in this translucency and I grew some of my own by holding a lighted match to "beds" of granular frost. Ferns, fronds and feathers were everywhere, with many Christmassy garlands; and how delighted I was to find the Tannenbaum, the fir tree, over and over again.

But now there was my own Christmas tree to discover, wood to carry, paths to shovel, evergreens to cut for decoration, river ice to break for water, more treats to find for the animals and birds I hoped would come to share them. I went spinning like a top from one inside job to another and then burst out the door into a world of wonder. So still, so white, so gloriously shining; so tall and vast, so utterly filled with snow and solitude. And I, this little I, in the middle of it all. O Life,

O Life, I kept saying, this is too much. You have made it all too beautiful. I can hardly bear it.

The snow still fell, but lightly now and I noticed that the flakes were smaller and simpler than the complex forms of yesterday. They had come from the highest clouds, the cirro and the cirrostratus, where lunar and solar halos originate. In fact, the halos are made by light passing through the ice crystals uninterruptedly, from one hexagonal face to another. Light, light, it seemed to run through me like a current that wakened to ecstasy every nerve and vein and sinew. I hugged myself with joy.

The snow stopped, but I didn't. I strung rose hip and western dogwood berries, popcorn I had grown and red huckleberries I had put down in jars. All for the young fir at the forest's edge which would be my living, growing Christmas tree.

Green cookies would go on it and golden doughnuts, scarlet apples, carrot candles, turnip and beet balls. I would share it with the birds, though already their own tree was decorated with suet, seeds in fat, seeds in honey and sunflower seeds alone for the jays and varied thrushes. There was always food on the feeding tray, but this was special.

No browse for the deer, for they were yarded up miles away and the snow between was deep. Porridge with sweet fruit in it for the old coyote, and stew for the wildcat who both came around for a handout, now and then. In case the old and almost toothless cougar arrived he would have both, a washbowl of it near the Christmas tree. The bears would be hibernating surely and the birds wouldn't start coming until dawn. Except for the owls, of course.

Just before dusk I went inside to stir up the fire, but I put on no lights. Munching a sandwich I sat down by the window to watch. The sky had cleared and behind Cougar Mountain the moon was rising. The snow sparkled wherever light touched it and the world outside was a child's dream story before life crumpled the page. But as the moon rose my hopes fell, for two hours had gone by and no guests had come to the feast. Would they come? Would there be a stranger among them to invoke the old Celtic blessing? "Often, often, often goes the Christ in the Stranger's guise."

Then a grey shadow stirred as the coyote sidled slowly out of the cabin's darker shade. He went to the big bowl of porridge placed on the kitchen side of the house, where he usually fed. At that moment I realized that the wildcat bowl was in use too—and was that a lean tawny movement near the forest woodpile? Were those the golden eyes of a great grey owl in the hemlock?

But I forgot them all when I spotted a furry from rolling up the path from the river. A bear, looking like a two-year-old. No, not the same one which had been romping up and down the river all summer, gorging himself on berries. That one had a sharper face. This one hardly seemed to notice his fellow diners, but headed straight for the bird tree—and honey.

I tore into the kitchen, opened a jar of fish and tossed this towards him. The coyote and wildcat jumped away, but came cautiously back again. While bruin was trying to get fish out of the snow I opened more jars. As he was on the seventh, the forest woodpile seemed to lengthen and the old cougar came out into the moonlight. In its kind glow he appeared almost young and invincible. The bear raised his head and looked at him. Then he grabbed up the last piece of fish and ambled rather hastily down the garden path. When I looked around my holiday table was empty, except for the ancient one enjoying his porridge-stew and I taking another sandwich out of my pocket.

But for a short while we had all been there, in peace and acceptance; cougar, coyote, wildcat, bear, owl and human. For those moments there had been something between us. A truce? No, more than that; a bond. I became truly part of all life then and for a flash I saw how earth might have been. I was not even startled; only surprised that they had not spoken and the old tales of animals talking on Christmas Eve come alive—again? But perhaps we did "talk" together. The stars glittered, the moon silver-coated the snow, the cougar and I ate. I felt that the others were not too far away, watching.

At least one of them came back, for next morning both trees were wrecks and it didn't look like owl work. But it didn't matter either. I fixed them up again before the birds arrived and Christmas Day feasting began.

That day was a dream of heaven, blue and white and shining. I went through it on wings and wings were all around me; chickadee, wren, kinglet, jay, kingfisher, blackbird, varied thrush, creeper, nuthatch, grosbeak, bunting, redstart, water ouzel and even a willow ptarmigan down from the peaks.

After dark, a pygmy owl hushed in, a saw-whet owl perched on my ridgepole and later still a horned owl came looking for mice that were looking for crumbs. Three of my four-footed friends returned, though not the bear. But he had played the Stranger's part and I was blessed indeed. Now I knew what door had opened and that it would never open for me again in just this way. I looked up at the mountains and the sapphire sky to say thank you, thank you. It seemed so pitifully little for all I had been given.

Wilderness Welcome

GUEST patterns in the wilderness have changed very little since pioneer days. Even in these pilfering times most of us who live in the mountain isolation of the Cascades leave our houses unlocked and the traveller who needs food and rest is welcome to both, whether we are at home or not. The only payment asked of him is that he leave things as he found them, replace any wood he used for fires and, in turn, keep open house for other wayfarers. Where I live travel is by foot only, so a meal is a must for all those who go through on the trails near my property.

My neighbours (the nearest one is four miles away) and I usually get both amusement and pleasure out of these visitors who come hunting gold, timber, fish or deer. What they think of us they're too polite to say—but we can guess! Our greatest enjoyment, however, is to go visiting among ourselves. This doesn't happen very often in summer because then we are either too busy with warm-weather chores or else we are being strenuously visited from "outside." Sometimes in spring and autumn it doesn't happen at all, except in the case of emergency, for these are our busiest seasons. They are the times of preparation, so that we may not be caught napping by bustling June or steel-jawed December.

But in winter the two families who belong to our little branch railroad can breathe easier. The worst rockslides are over and if the road closes down until June—as it sometimes does—there will be no need to patrol the track in howling blizzards or to stumble through shoulder-high drifts on some midnight emergency. Those of us who raise food for the rest or who have "retired" to the round-the-clock work of wilderness living can relax a little after the fall rush to fill root house and cellar. Now there is only snow to shovel and wood to cut—plus the thousand and one small jobs which have been piling up during the busy days.

Good as our gossip grapevine is we haven't been able to perfect it to the extent of telling who is coming to visit us and when. There is only one telephone for the whole district and that is many miles from my cabin. So one winter morning I may hear a shout from across the river and look out to see a neighbour standing on the cage platform. Clustered around the platform ladder are his entire family and sometimes their neighbours, packs on their backs or bundles in their arms. Rarely there are as many as six, and as I throw on my windbreaker and well-oiled boots I hastily do some mental arithmetic—which always leads to the same answer: that some of us will have to sleep on the floor. For anyone who arrives after breakfast is expected to be still with us for that meal the next day. If he comes before that hour then we figure that he wants to get back home before dark.

I unhook the cage so it can be pulled over to the other side by the pulley rope and, two by two, my guests get on it and come sliding along the cable towards me. It is a scene which might have been torn out of an old volume of pioneer days. Behind me is my mountain-guarded valley piled high with snow which has sifted down on every last twig and drifted deep into the great forest at my front door. Directly at my back is the clearing with root house, woodshed and bark-covered cabin from which smoke rises straight and blue into the frosty air. I am standing on a wooden platform at the river's edge with the Teal running narrow and dark in front of me. Ice has nearly covered this wide mountain stream and now it flows almost without a sound between high white banks. There is whiteness and silence everywhere. Even the voices of my visitors sound small and frail in this immensity of mountain wilderness. As they come towards me on the cage they are dwarfed to midget size by the great backdrop of Fireweed Mountain, sparkling with sun against the cloudless blue sky.

"Hello!" they cry as they dismount on my platform. "We thought we'd come and spend the day with you."

Soon we are all walking along the path to my cabin between waistdeep snowbanks. As we speak to each other our breath floats silver on the keen air and the snow crunches sharply under our feet. But the cabin is cosy with fire and snow-banked walls. In a few moments woollen clothes are drying on a pole over the oil drum heater and every inch of space is littered with food and bedding. My guests have brought blankets, pie, cake, cookies, fruit, a haunch of venison and some bear steaks. They have even packed in old newspapers to start my fire and some special delicacies they thought I might like: lemon butter, homemade fudge, a small bottle of elderberry cordial. Sometimes they bring me some stewing meat of mountain goat or a brace of Franklin's grouse kept fresh in our community deep freeze locker, the great outdoors.

Throughout the day we consume quantities of food, tell yeasty yarns and recount neighbourhood gossip. There is much laughter and hearty good fellowship as we detail our plans for the working season to come and receive unabashed criticism of them. The children build snowmen and play with workshop scraps until they are almost too tired to eat supper. There is little drinking at any of our gatherings; usually just a small glass of wine, rum or whiskey before the main meal. Cocktails are looked upon as an effete concoction, far too weak to fortify anyone against wilderness weather. There are several heavy drinkers among us, but they usually reserve their sprees for trips to the city or to the nearest village nearly thirty miles away.

That's probably why we seem to enjoy the village square dances so much more than the other people there, for our whole community goes down to them and so we consider ourselves as being still "at home." We don't go very often, but when we do we make a night of it and have something to talk about for weeks. The children are bedded down on the floor of an adjoining room and the rest of us "alamain left and circle all" until breakfast time.

When I go visiting I feel as though I were walking through the pages of *Pioneer Life in Canada* or some kindred book. My pack is big with food and workshop toys. When I shall be seeing neighbours who haven't many trees nearby I sometimes make a separate pack of pitchwood for quick, hot fires. That takes me back to a winter night farther east when I opened my cabin door to find two near neighbours and their three children on the snowy steps. The father held two giant blocks of maple, the mother carried stove-length fir logs, the two elder children had balsam and spruce, while the toddler staggered in with an armful of cedar kindling. We sat around the heater and talked until it was all gone except the two maple logs—and they warmed me until daylight.

After I cross the Teal River I have half a mile of fairly level forest trail to traverse before I start climbing the switchbacks of Fireweed Mountain. If the snow is very deep I use bear paws (small, round snowshoes) as skis are no good in the thick bush. But it is when there is only a light sprinkling of snow over rain-frozen ground that the going is really grim and my backsliding terrific. I remember journeys when the whole mountain seemed to be coated with ice. It was impossible to keep my feet so I crawled on hands and knees, pulling myself along by tree and stone. Going down I skidded from tree to tree and on one eventful occasion I lost control altogether and arrived at the bottom with the whole seat torn out of my ski pants!

On still another winter day, without snowshoes, I struggled through three miles of shoulder-high snow; a tiny speck wading painfully through high, white seas. That was one of the three times when, for a fleeting and cowardly moment, I thought I might never arrive anywhere on this earth. The other two occasions were when I was lost in mountain mist and a mountain snowstorm. I shall not easily forget them— nor shall I forget the wilderness welcome of my neighbours at the end of those adventurous trails.

Logic out of Eden

IF YOU HEAR first cousin's cousin to an atomic explosion up in these mountains some day soon you'll know that I've been told once too often that women are inferior to men. The "dudes" who come in are the worst offenders, but the disease seems to be pretty well distributed wherever you go. Anyone who lives with animals knows how artificial is our whole "civilized" conception of male and female. It's too long a subject to deal with here, but when summer's over and the outsiders have gone home I do a bit of thinking about it.

I think it was Socrates who said and Montaigne who endorsed him: "I look on all men as my compatriots." I shall give both these savants the benefit of the doubt and believe that by "men" they meant "man" and not simply the masculine animal. They were wise enough to, but most people of today—and of any day so far—have not their discernment. Even those who believe that Eve was formed from Adam's rib seem to repudiate that very theory by the vigour with which they contend that these twain are *not* one flesh; that men are men and women are women, while woe betide those who declare that they are simply and foremost human beings. What stern wedges they drive between male and female. What odious comparisons they draw to prove some fancied difference. Like Dorian, I "have seen a more formidable storm in a boiling saucepan," for I claim that there are no differences, spiritually or mentally, between men and women except those built up by superstition, self-interest and stupidity.

The war between the sexes is as needless and costly as any campaign of any conqueror. It has caused more suffering than any other one thing in the world. If it were not so tragic it would be ridiculous. Instead of companionship in marriage or out of it there are such feints, thrusts and parries as might be employed by two keen-eyed mice circling warily around a scrap of cheese. One thing is certain: they are never going to sit down on their haunches and eat that cheese together. Pitifully few of us ever consider anyone without bias, but in the case of women the scales are so loaded against them that any true estimate is impossible. She is a woman, therefore she is "uncertain, coy and hard to please"—and every other shibboleth which has been invented by the conquering male and the catering female. For they are both equally guilty. Those of us who wish everyone to be judged by merit and not by antecedent or precedent are so much in the minority that our squeaks of protest go unheard above the shouts of: "'And never the twain shall meet'—except biologically!"

Women are supposed to be greater gossips than men, but when men are together with those of their own sex they yield the palm to no one. Gossip has two intertwined roots: envy and a feeling of inferiority. As women have always been made to feel inferior to men that may be why they delight in tales which give them a sense of superiority, both over their unfortunate victims and their uninformed listeners. Men often feel inferior to other men and so compete to hold the floor, if only for a short interval, with a spicy yarn concerning mutual acquaintances. Or perhaps everyone else is doing it and it's part of "being a good fellow." If they did not feel inferior there would be no reason for being anything but themselves.

Women's work, men's work; women's ways, men's ways—what unparallelled nonsense! Given the same conditioning and opportunities there would soon be no discernable mental difference between male and female, while the disparity in their physical strength is of little importance in a machine age. So what remains? Oh, yes, child-bearing. Medical science and some judicious making and breaking of economic and legal fixations could easily provide that no woman need be penalized for her share in perpetuating life—even though as the world is today, it might be a matter of controversy whether her work in this case was really worthwhile. As to the effect of child-bearing on mental status: I refuse to judge the character and intelligence of any man or woman by the ability to obey a call of nature.

When I read in English, American and Canadian newspapers about men tearing off with top awards in cooking and embroidery at various fairs, I begin to wonder if a more efficient world wouldn't do a lot of job-changing between the sexes. The best cooks, the greatest talkers, the worst gossips and the most confirmed sentimentalists I know are all men. But some of the worst traitors I know to their own sex are women. There will be, as usual, male and female howls of rage at these opinions of mine—but I have lots of good company in them. Norman Cousins, editor emeritus of the famous *Saturday Review of Literature*, would know what I was talking about and so would the various groups of men who have banded together on this continent to try to raise the legal and economic status of women. I don't know how many of them are mountain men, but their ideas are right at home in the wilderness.

Perhaps we're just too simple up here. Women are human beings to us and we judge them, as we do men, by the way they cope with a tough country. We know here that how a man makes out depends more on his wife than himself. Every now and then a crisis comes up and we see a woman show enough courage and savvy to make a man wonder where *he* was all the time. We don't put women up on a pedestal just because it's high and we give them a helping hand if they slip into muddy water. We neither flatter nor belittle them. If they're able to swing it alone and pull together, too, then they're part of our mountain life and on the same level with all of us. There is no room here for weaklings, male or female, and still less for anyone who believes in religious, racial, colour or sex superiority. We know that only the man or woman who is unsure feels that way—and this is no country for the uncertain, spiritually or physically.

January Jaunt

EVERY NOW and then I do something to which my neighbours refer as "the craziest thing ever" and which I call an adventure. Some people break out in a rash when their blood becomes too rich with the heavy diet of winter; I break out in such escapades as this. After it is all over I go back to safe and sane living with a very satisfied—I almost said smug—feeling. Once more I have done something dangerous; but something I wanted to do very much, that satisfied a demand in me.

One such "adventure," shortly after I came to my valley, really hardly deserves that term for it was a very mild affair indeed. It all began with an entirely brash idea on my part that it would be easy walking along the shores of the Teal when the January ice stretched far out into the river. The wind kept all but two or three inches of snow cleared away from it and it seemed to me a simple matter to ice-walk the six miles along the Teal and the mile over Sable Mountain which would take me to a Sunday dinner at my neighbour's. I could have gone much more easily by way of Main Street and Village Road, but that seemed tame and ordinary compared to the river way which I had never tried. It was going to be good fun—"you have the funniest ideas of fun," said my neighbour later—and I could hardly wait to start.

When Sunday came it was a cold, clear, blue and golden day, with a few heavy clouds which I ignored. I slung my pack on my back (an invitation to a wilderness meal in winter means you are asked for the night and no one arrives without a gift of food) and went whistling down the path between the shoulder-high snow banks. I was allowing myself three hours to get there, which seemed ample time even if the going got heavy. I looked along the Teal as I pulled across and as far as I could see—which was about half a mile—the ice seemed thick, with the snow on it shallow and unobstructed.

That's exactly the way it was—for half a mile. The lovely song of the water ouzel mingled with river music as I walked. The woods were fairyland, for there had been a heavy fall of snow the night before and even the smallest twig was swathed in white fox. Snow crystals flashed and glimmered, chickadees were sibilant in the underbrush, great white peaks towered around me—and I was part of all this beauty! Just to walk through such a world on such a day seemed reason enough for living.

I had gone almost a mile before I struck the first big pile of driftwood. Up until then I had been following the tracks of a big dog coyote which had apparently navigated the pile easily, but I was too heavy for that. I went back into the bush and found the snow far deeper there than I had anticipated. In Home Wood the trees are so large and the overhead so dense that there is never more than a foot or two of snow at the very most. But parts of the opposite bank of the Teal have been logged off heavily and so now it is both more open and bushier. However, although the going was hard it didn't seem too long before I was striding along the ice again. The clouds were spreading, I noticed.

The second driftwood pile I managed to clamber over, as

the logs were bigger and at least held me up—although they were so slippery that my feet were more often off than on them. I said words because I had not worn caulk boots. But even those wouldn't have helped when I came to the third heap of river-piled trunks and branches. It had water on each side of it, and stretched out into the swift centre current of the river. On the land side it went back and back into the open woods where the snowdrifts were up to my waist and sometimes higher. To go around it was the only possible manoeuvre as where it lay on solid ground it stretched for a tangled, foot-trapping eighth of a mile. The sun had gone now and the air was grey.

I don't know whether you have ever walked through very deep snow. It isn't walking, really, it is wading. There is the same swing of the body you use when ploughing through water and the same sensation of fighting an inert mass. It is very tiring and the cold seeps through your garments into your very bones. If you struggle through it long enough you begin to wonder if there will ever be an end. You look around and see nothing but deep snow everywhere. Then you know that you must go on or you will die.

I couldn't get out to the river again for beyond that point of land there was no beach and no ice; just a steep bank falling into deep water and woods piled high with drifts. Owing to the curve of the Teal at this point all the gravel shore and ice was on the other side of the river. I didn't know the country then, and I hadn't thought of that. Of course I should have turned back, but I didn't. I went on until the snow began to fall again, and then it was too late to retreat. I lost all track of distance or of time. I only knew that I must put one foot forward, and then the other one somehow. That I must not panic. That I must not stop too long to rest or perhaps I would never start again.

Finally, the moment arrived when I realized it was quite hopeless to try and walk along the flat as far as the trail which struck up Sable Mountain. I must try to make the half mile on the level, and the half mile straight up to Village Road while I still had enough strength and before the trail was blotted out by snow. I wasn't lost, but that could certainly happen if I didn't get on more familiar ground before the short day closed in.

Fireweed, Goat and Sable Mountains have been burned over so often that there is no real timber left on any of them. They are great slopes of rock and gravel with huge boulders, and small bushes here and there. Only where the trail runs from Village Road over Sable would there be any real shelter for me. With a light snowfall these open places are nothing at all to worry about, but in this... I had one very cowardly moment of wondering whether I was going to get through alive before I determined that I certainly was.

I didn't climb up that mountain, I crawled. The snow was up to my armpits; I could spread my arms out flat at my sides as though I were treading water. There was no hope of taking a decent step; all I could do was throw myself forward as though breasting surf, dig my arms deep in the snow, and pull myself up a little at a time. Sometimes a big boulder or a pile of rock would make progress faster by giving me something solid by which to pull myself along. But halfway up the going got so steep that I couldn't follow a straight line any more: I had to switchback. Up until then I had been able to see my tracks behind me, but now the snow began to fall so heavily that every mark was blotted out almost as soon as it was made. I was alone in a white, swirling world. The snow stung my eyes so that I had to slit them to see at all. But of what use were my eyes when everything looked the same?

Yet I made it. I can't tell you how. There seems to be a blank in there; probably because everything had been blotted from my mind except the grim determination to go on. I still had sense enough to recognize the slight levelling out of Village Road at the point where I struck it, and strength enough to follow it until I came to an alder grove where the snow was shallower, and I could rest a while in semi-shelter. But not for long. When the dagger of the wind began to prick through my clothes I knew I must move on again. But moving wasn't easy. Even that short halt had stiffened me and as my body cooled I could feel where the snow had soaked through my tenderfoot clothing. Darkness had come down, and how easy it would have been to lie down in the snow and rest—and rest...

It wasn't until I was sitting in front of the Trantor's stove with a hot drink in my hand, and my feet in a tub of hot water—prescribed by Mrs. Trantor for the pneumonia she was quite sure I was going to have—that I fully realized what might have happened. No one knew that I had started, no one thought anything of the fact I hadn't arrived. The Trantors had wondered a bit, but concluded that I just couldn't get away. They never used Village Road themselves in the winter as they were not far from the railroad tracks which run along the flank of Sable below their house. Certainly they would never have dreamed that even a wilderness greenhorn could be so mad as to deliberately go off the trail in winter, and without snowshoes.

So if I had lain down in the soft snow to rest I might not have been found until spring. I think it was that thought which hit me hardest. Spring—and I not here to see it! The birds coming back, and I not alive to welcome them! I knew then, fully, how lucky I had been. I have been really lost since, once in snow, and once in mist. I have faced boiling rapids and wild animals many times, and been close enough to death to feel the first chill touch me. But this January jaunt was a foolish affair—and I wouldn't have missed it for all the chimney corners in Vancouver!

Moon of the Great Cold

"SNOW LIKE meal, snow a great deal," the old saying has it and it is in January that it comes true. As Janus, the two-faced, turns towards the New Year, white silence closes down on forest and clearing with only a secret whispering from rivers running low between icy banks. When a tree cracks with frost, usually in the deep night stillness, I feel the report must be loud enough to be heard around the world. How splendid, indeed, if it could be: this natural sound drowning out the artificial clamour of guns and bureaucrats.

Sometimes the snow falls gently as content; sometimes it is driven dementedly before a wind that whirls down mountain passes and strides arrogantly across my clearing, with bushes and trees and even the smoke from my chimney bowing before it. Gradually great bosses form between the branches of fir and balsam, cedar and hemlock. They melt and fall and form again while, as the month goes on, slender saplings lean farther and farther towards the ground in an obeisance that often becomes permanent. Stumps put on their tall white shakos, and in the open places around them wind patterns the snow like watered silk or like beach sand after the tide goes out.

This is the surface tale, but underneath snow and ice there

is a different story. Beetles sleep beneath a leaf and chinchbugs slumber among old grasses. On the withered heads of mullein are egg cases of spiders and cocoons of butterflies. In the soil itself you will find leaf-hoppers, weevils, ants, aphis lions and eggs of crickets. On trees and bushes there will be various beetles, plant lice, oyster scale and, unfortunately for this gardener, numerous other pests. Bees, wasps, flies and mosquitos are wintering in fences, woodpiles and buildings. Leeches have burrowed into the mud or crept under stones. Whole communities of insects and amphibians hibernate beneath that fluffy white blanket upon which, with its air spaces and lightness, certain Scottish weavers have modelled their own products.

Because the upper layers of soil which have been covered by soft snow seldom fall below freezing, there is safety for those eggs which the grasshoppers laid just below ground surface when the sun was warm with summer. Ice is an insulator too and beneath it a complex and active January life goes on. Rainbow and brook trout seem to find plenty to feed on—mayfly nymphs, dragonflies, snails, water fleas, roundworms—in both of my rivers. In fact the brook trout, lurking in pools and backwaters, reach the end of their October-January spawning season now. But it will take spring to hatch their eggs, for mid-winter cold slows all development of life.

The newts and salamanders I last spied basking in autumn sun, may have decided to go underground beneath the ice and feed on insect larvae. The frogs too, and it is possible to find large numbers of tadpoles in nature's cold frames. All life moves downward. Here and there in the woods small pipe holes in the snow mark the entrance and exit of the ground squirrel's passageway. My friends, the black bears, dig in under windfalls and overhanging rocks or pre-empt a cave if they can find one. All of them except that young bear with the wanderlust who continues to leave his tracks in my cold woods. I am convinced he belongs to the same travelling family as the yearling who spent one whole summer recently romping up and down Wren River with rolling abandon.

Whatever the bears may be doing—or even the skunks, who like to wander around on mild days—the chipmunks and bats seem to be sound asleep. Deer and some rats have performed their annual migrations down the mountains and the former are now drifting along the Teal to their winter yarding place. Even the invertebrates and amphibians have made what seem like great migrations to them: from tree top to ground, from leaf litter to below the soil, from land to water. Toads and snakes are almost completely dormant and all the hibernators have put on extra layers of fat to see them through the winter. You should have seen the bears stuffing themselves last fall!

Ptarmigans, weasels and rabbits have turned white now because old Mother Nature knows that light colours are better insulators against both heat and cold than dark ones. Also it makes it harder for enemies to spot these small creatures, especially when they have a tail-streak of black as do the snow bunting, ptarmigan and weasel. The eye is caught by this and usually fails to see the rest of the body.

The rabbits, far from sleeping, use these winter nights to play in the moonlight. Their diet, like that of the deer, has changed from fresh plants to bark and twigs. The deer mouse digs tunnels lined with flakes and leaves his tiny marks beside every trail I follow. Some mouse families are raising their infants now, judging by the holes in my new flannelette sheets.

The bobcats pad by on spectral snowshoes, sometimes over

those underground chambers where several snakes lie coiled one around another. Mink, otter and marten slip along the water's edge in their rich dark coats and thickly-clad coyotes escort me secretly on winter journeys. So does Grandpa Cougar, who is still alive, but has—to judge by the lighter imprints of his great pads—lost considerable weight. With meat the price it is and venison getting scarcer every year, I can't afford to open a butcher shop for him. All I can do is wish him a quick, painless death while he still has brain and brawn. I could even wish that he might find it at my hand— the hand of a friend.

The winter wren, chickadee, varied thrush and other birds which winter here have grown an undercoat of small downy feathers—beneath their outer feathers, which now overlap more—to keep out cold and wet. Visitors such as the evening and pine grosbeak, the redpoll and the snow bunting pass through, moving towards the coast—where recent winters have fooled even wise old birds. But the grouse just grow feather snowshoes and hang around my valley, diving into the snow beneath a protecting tree for warmth and hiding. Sunflower, squash, pumpkin and many wild plant seeds are in the feeding trays now, with nut meats and venison suet stuck in the rough bark of Douglas firs.

Like bear, coyote, bobcat and bird, I have put on heavier clothing too, although mine seems to bear no relation to down at the moment. Like my sleepyhead skunk family I spend longer hours in bed and, in fact, do considerable hibernating in my own peculiar way. The small branch railroad is closed down until May and miles of snow lie between me and my neighbours. Now is the time of rest and preparation so that there may be a lovelier spring.

But not too much rest. There are many jobs to do before

April comes pirouetting through my valley and so many things to see outside also. Buds to examine, seed pods to put under the magnifying glass, nests of the tree squirrel to look for in crotches of trees or on top of vacated owl nests. Not to mention the owls themselves: the great horned, pigmy, hawk or screech, sometimes the beautiful snowy owl (when lemmings are scarce up north) and others less photogenic, but all with those immovable hypnotic eyes which Indians liken to the morning star.

Sometimes I discover a bat hibernating in a hollow tree or the burrow of a mouse under an old stump. Stumps and rotting logs are wonderful places to find centipedes, beetles, flies, spiders and various other small residents of my valley. Sometimes I come across moth cocoons and hibernating butterflies in ground litter by old windfalls. Worms are usually one floor lower down. Truly, it seems that there isn't a square foot of ground, a grass stem, a tree trunk, a plant or a building that isn't acting as a winter residence for some form of wildlife—including me.

When someone asks: "Whatever do you do with yourself down there all winter?" or "Don't the quiet and inactivity drive you crazy?" I say: "Friend, it's never been quiet enough for me to hear a deer mouse snore and anyway I'd be too busy to notice." Whoever called winter the dead time of year ought to visit me for a while. I'd show them lots of life in the Moon of the Great Cold.

February Fires

THIS IS THE month the sun comes back, peering through the gap between Cougar and Evergreen with that golden glance which quickens the pulse of the world. But February is also the time of the deepest snow, the fiercest blizzards, the most crackling cold. It is the month of Kichi, the Big Moon; of stars that spark my valley with light and dazzle my eyes with their cold brilliance. It is the time of greatest silence. Each flake that has fallen since October has led to this muffling of forest and river and clearing as though the very snow itself were soundproof.

Even the coyotes—on the move now that the drifts are deep, and food is hard to get—are only darker silences drifting through the brush. The dri-ki trees (fire- or water-killed timber that is still standing) on Fireweed Mount pose gaunt and still against the slope's vivid whiteness. Above them, after darkness, the northern lights do Indian dances, but their swift rushes and retreats are audible to no human ear. Soundlessly the buckskinned hunters of the sky follow the Great Bear, Orion watches the bull-bulk of Taurus, and Sirius, the Dog Star, stands guard upon the Hydra. And just as soundlessly I stand upon my knoll wrapped in the blessed comforter of peace.

Around me on the snow move the unheard shadows of the conifers. Cedar branches resemble a fern designed in lace, delicate hemlock boughs have their outlines blurred like an out-of-focus negative. Pine branches reflect in a rosette pattern, huckleberry bushes are shadowed into great bunches of flowers. But when the moon or stars etch a fir bough on the snow the result is strong and dark and compact, though sometimes with a sweep and a curve to it that reminds me of ostrich feathers.

Pine branches are the most beautiful when burning. The long needles turn into glowing tassels of golden thread which looks as soft as silk. Soon these are overlaid with a delicate grey tissue through which the gold pulses like a beating heart. Fir and hemlock have their swan song of beauty also as needles become rosettes of flame which shimmer and fade along the twigs, transforming each one into a garland for some fire queen's shining hair.

When I go up the Wren to sleep out on a February night just for the fun of it, the flames from my campfire twist up like glowing wires which throw off dancing sparks as they are blown higher and higher by the fire's hot breath. Back of the flames is a rock wall which will reflect their heat, but if I cannot find one I make a low reflector of green logs.

More wood is stacked close by, for that is the first consideration of the winter camper; enough fuel to last until daylight at least, and some dry twigs and bark under shelter so that if the fire goes out it may be easily started again. You never know—especially in February—when a blizzard may come howling down the mountain passes to make wood-hunting a hard and perhaps even a dangerous job. So the off-rose of cedar, the saffron of rotting hemlock, the clear ivory of fir glow softly against their snowy background as my night pile of firewood grows.

A standing dead tree burns better than timber that has been lying on the ground, but the balsam boughs I cut for bed and shelter must be green. I cut ten poles also, thrusting one end of each into the snow on a slant; five to a side and opposite each other. Then I pull each pair towards me and lash the free ends together with cedar fibre, giving me the walls of my shelter with an opening as large as I want it. Over the poles I pile evergreen branches, build up a balsam bed at least two feet thick and throw my sleeping-bag down on it; usually with a deerskin or a ground sheet underneath to act as a cold-breaker by night as it protects my pack from melting snow by day. Now, with the heat of the fire reflected through my doorway I shall be as snug as any bug burrowed down below the frost line.

The smoke from my blaze filters through the forest, bringing out into the eerie, disembodied relief of firelight those parts of the trees which it does not cover. Sometimes it begins to climb, quickly and steadily, moving up the mountain beside me with an ease which I envy. In one deep dusk this high smoke caught the last rays of the sun setting on the Wren uplands, and became the saffron veil of some mysterious houri. One clear, cold night the first rays of an invisible moon transmitted it into a great cobweb of silver and crystal which surely had been spun by stars and not by fire at all. As the logs settle down to steady burning, flamelight stalks through the aisles of the forest to capture other and smaller glows which tell me that I am not alone.

Sometimes it is the yellow glow of an owl's eyes as he flits like another smoke eddy between the trees or sits immovable upon a bough. I remember an old-timer telling me that if I walked around an owl in the same direction long enough it would twist its head off trying to follow me with its eyes. But really it only turns its head as far as possible in one direction, and then swivels it round in the other with such speed that it seems to be one continuous motion going the same way.

The pupils of an owl's eyes expand in darkness and contract in light like those of the cat family. They can't move their eyeballs, however, and so must turn their whole heads when they want to look in another direction. Some owls—such as the snowy and burrowing—can not only see well by day, but like to go hunting then. Others, such as the Richardson's, are so blind in daylight that several times I have walked right up to one and touched it.

As I lie down on my balsam bed the death squeak of a mouse sounds in the still wood, and I know that the great grey owl—which I last glimpsed sitting on a nearby stump in wooden Indian pose—has moved swiftly and surely. In the morning there will be small pellets of fur and bone on the snow: the indigestible and so disgorged parts of the mouse which had been swallowed whole.

Tomorrow I may find anything from sunbathing spiders to a woolly bear caterpillar wandering over the snow. There may even be butterflies enjoying a February thaw on a stump steaming with solar warmth—or frostfire smoke, as we call it. As I brew my breakfast coffee in a tin pail and flip my sourdough flapjacks I know I'll see at least one water ouzel doing setting up exercises, and more than one winter wren with tail industriously twitching and a beady eye cocked for crumbs.

But tonight I shall look for nothing but dreamless sleep as my campfire makes torches for the moon to walk by silver trails. I pile some thick, long-burning bark on the flames, wash in melted snow, and crawl into my warmed bed. The cold fire of February stars glitter above the tree tops, shadows dance around me, and silence is my slumber song.

February Footnotes

WHAT DELIGHTFUL colours there are in a February thaw! The white of snow, the many shadings of conifer green, the amethyst of deciduous trees, the blue of brush fire smoke, the brown of bark. Evergreen acquires a crest of silver in daylight, with leafless trees drifting towards it like purple incense and below them the pearl of heavier mist. Across my valley the smoke from my chimney runs like an unleashed greyhound leaping to the north.

The days come so close to you out here in the wilderness. Some nestle confidingly in the heart, others stride by with a gay wave of wing or branch, many come openhanded as a friend. But however they arrive they are my comrades. In the city, days seem removed, apart. They are a bank account to be totalled or a grocery basket to be filled. Sometimes they creak and jostle and look at you in a hostile fashion. You are never quite sure of them; you can never quite relax in their company.

The mountain nights are lovely also; not only the nights of blazing moonlight on snow, the timid nights of spring or the full-lipped ones of summer—but any night. It may be a dark night of February thaw like this, but there will be the rivers murmuring of the snow melting in the mountains, and the winds telling of the patches of bare earth where the sun is warm and golden. There will be the scent of snow and bracken drifting in the window—and solitude. Solitude so complete that you can hear your dreams coming softly through the forest and over the hills of spring.

Now there is a hiatus in time: winter is nearly over, spring has not quite begun. I feel suspended in time, as though I belonged to nothing and were going nowhere. It is a good feeling. Although my physical radius is more and more restricted as the rains pour down and the trails become slippery with ice, yet my spiritual radius grows larger and larger until at last I realize that I belong to the whole universe and not just to one little planet in it.

I believe very strongly that it would be an excellent thing for the world if everyone could be isolated in this way for some period of their lives; if they had to face themselves honestly and live with themselves companionably; if they had time for contemplation, for friendship with nature and with "breath, the neighbour." To be able to stand aside like this and look on the world whole and not just in part is a wonderful gift from life. I know how lucky I am and I treasure each moment of these quiet days; for once a day has gone who can say if its like will ever come again? These years of mountain living have been the happiest of my life. There is such deep satisfaction in the simple, natural, physical things of this existence and in having the time and solitude in which to cultivate the life of the mind. How fortunate I am to have been able to live the life I love! So few people ever can—and fewer still will be able to in the crowded, robot earth years to come.

In February a provident nature is at a premium in my valley. Anything can happen: rockslides may close trails and railroad, my cage platforms may go down with the floods, or the cable across the Teal snap with alternate warmth and cold. Then packing supplies would be impossible and to go "outside" I would have to walk over trailess mountains for days before I could hope to reach the first settlement on my side of the river or the first bridge across it. So I rejoice in my full root house and cellar, in the herbs drying in the attic, in all the supplies of necessity and comfort which I grew and made or—rarely—bought for myself in the good weather. I would not like to imagine what might happen to a person who did not plan ahead in this sort of life—and there have been many such. Some survived, some died. It is amazing the number of people who seem to find something glamorous and charming about improvident individuals. Not I. We wilderness dwellers have little use for those who use the hard-earned savings or provisions of others because they haven't had enough sense and strength of character to save for themselves.

I think of this especially when I have gone "outside" and picked up a bad flu germ or, as happened once, sprained my ankle. If it hadn't been for the food I had stocked in the house for just such an emergency I would have had a very thin time indeed. Luckily all such emergencies have arrived in winter to date, so that I could melt snow for water without too much difficulty. But when they do come I react to them very much as an animal would. When an animal is sick it goes off by itself and dozes, for days sometimes. It eats very little or not at all. I have always believed that nature was the best doctor for me. That means eliminating all strain, inside and out, so that the entire energy can go into getting well. Certainly a terrific amount of energy is drained away from us, sick or well, by conversation, noise and disturbance. Solitude and silence—my two physicians! They have cured not only my body but my soul.

I have proved this physical healing for myself not just in one instance, but in many. Perhaps I have proved it most when I have gone against my own instincts and adhered to the conventional idea of being fussed over when ill. Then it seemed as though I were like an aircraft which had gone off the radio beam. I was uneasy, anxious, and it was not until I had discovered the cause and applied the remedy that I could be tranquil again. Then I had the satisfied feeling of one who has come back on course once more. Of course I realize that this regime of mine can take the place of neither medicine nor surgery when things have gone too far. But such a regime and faith together might work a miracle of prevention. I have always believed that faith can do anything. Yet there is a hitch to that also: how many of us have *enough* faith?

The bears of my valley will soon be out, gaunt and hungry. They will make straight for the young shoots of yellow arum, salmonberry and bracken. They know that is what their bodies need. We call this instinct—I have so named it myself many times—buy I wonder if that is the right expression. Is it not rather the perception of a fact? The impoverished body added to the herbs are the two and two which make four. We have come so far from the animals in this way and from such perceptions that we are prone to place the whole matter in a sort of dream world. We dissociate the word "instinct" from common sense and to most of us it has a vague, unpredictable connotation. Frankly I think it is about as ethereal as a flapjack. It means the ability to recognize and act upon a state of affairs. Just that.

So when the bears and other animals begin hunting for those young shoots it's going to be just too bad if there are not enough greens to go round. I want my share as usual or there'll be trouble!

Wings in my Valley

ONE MORNING, just as the bright ribbons of sunrise began to unroll across the sky, a song sparrow burst into song. That is the only way I can describe that sudden, bright lyric of notes. I had heard it every spring and summer morning for years, but always accompanied by the plump chirp of robins, the chain notes of warblers, the shriek of the belted kingfisher or the whistle of my favourite hermit thrush. Now all of these were absent. Not a bird twittered. Not a feather stirred. Only that pure and lovely song coming from the underbrush a few yards from where I stood.

Again and again it came. Listening to it I looked around at the beauty of the mountain morning and knew that whatever others thought I lacked, I possessed all that really mattered. Even if I should lose every material thing, yet nothing could ever take away from me these dawns with the clouds glowing over Evergreen and a song sparrow carolling in the light. Nor the days of sun and flowers when I hear a rustling in the underbrush and look up from my work to see a plump brown bird with a nervous tail and darkly-streaked breast sitting on a stump not far away. Nor the evenings when the sun goes down behind Fireweed and the valley pulls up cool green sheets in readiness for the song sparrow's lullaby and sleep.

Yes, each day my valley is filled with song and each hour lilts by to the heart's own music of happiness. A downy woodpecker usually starts drilling industriously not long after breakfast and at intervals as I work I look up to see this small black and white carpenter with the back of his neck so badly sunburned, jabbing away at one of my firs or stopping to peer down at me with a bright, knowing look. I am always delighted to meet him for I know that when he is around a lot of harmful insects won't be. He is a particular enemy of the obnoxious tent caterpillar moth and so am I.

Sometimes Mrs. Franklin Grouse comes to sit on my roof or meets me on the trail with her children toddling just behind her tail. After a late, cold spring or a winter when the usually numerous rock rabbits of the district are scarce the grouse family may consist of only one or two brown babies, but in other years I have come across as many as eighteen infants peeping anxiously in their mother's wake.

Old Jim, a neighbour of mine, speaks of two kinds of grouse in the valley: blue and willow. These seem to be the common names for these birds in many districts. By the former he means the bird I call Franklin's and by the latter the ruffed grouse. But however they are called they have been good friends to me and I am always glad when I hear that wild, free drumming of the ruffed grouse in the forest or find Mrs. Franklin eyeing me from a stump in my clearing. There are no quail in my valley that I have seen, but down near the village all sorts of small infants and their mothers can be observed in the underbrush, while autumn brings great whirrings through the trees.

Once, coming along a sunny trail, I spied Mrs. Ruffed Grouse well ahead of me with several babies teetering along under the shelter of her broad tail. Papa Grouse had, as usual, gone about his own business by this time and the care and protection of her offspring rested on Mama alone. Hearing my approach and quite sure that I had designs on her darlings, she ran brokenly across my path and down the mountainside. So I looked *up* the mountain for her children and there they were, like small feathered stones frozen to the ground. All except one. He, poor baby, was frantically trying to dig himself into no space at all between two rocks. His little legs worked like pistons and his tiny rear agitated wildly. Fearing that he might put his small and addled head into a fatal place, I lifted him up gently and placed him on open ground. He stayed there, unmoving and almost unbreathing, just as I had put him down. I went away from there very quickly!

The Calliope and Rufous hummingbirds love to sit on my clothesline. Strangely enough for such active little creatures, they often perch there for several moments, swaying back and forth as the line stirs in the breeze. In years when urgent tasks keep me from getting the window boxes filled and set up at the usual time, the hummers fly from window to window positively glaring at me through each one. Sometimes they peck at the glass with angry bills and I know that those boxes had better be in place tomorrow or there will be neighbour trouble.

The bright red and iridescent green of these small creatures make my valley vibrate with colour all through the summer, and their flight is sheer poetry. Backwards, forwards, sideways they go or hover in the air like miniature helicopters. They look like birds and they act like insects, which makes them all the more interesting. It is good to hear a high, sharp *zing* and glance up to see a Rufous male hovering above a patch of delphinium and looking like an animated rosy flower himself. But by June there are no males left in my valley. Whether they begin their southern migration so early or follow the flowers up the mountains I have never found out. At any rate, Mesdames Rufous and Caliope are grass widows and very quarrelsome it makes them. Hardly an hour goes by without darts, hisses and then a furious rising in the air by two small creatures seemingly intent on exterminating each other. They argue over one scarlet lychnis when there are hundreds from which to choose. They jostle each other away from the petunias in the window boxes and their manners at the glass feeding tube—filled with honey and water—have to be seen to be believed. All is not sweetness and light in my Eden.

On my trips up the mountains surrounding the valley to see if I can locate the renegade hummer husbands, I usually find a Canada jay at each camping place. That funny fellow—who shares with the black bear the nickname of "clown of the woods"—goes through his whole bag of tricks for me as I sit by my solitary campfire beside some alpine lake or waterfall. He snaps up every scrap of food thrown to him and even pecks at my soap and tries to thrust his head into pot or frying pan. My prospector friends call him Whiskey Jack, Moose Bird (because he likes game offal), Camp Robber and considerably worse. But we two solitary birds understand each other and I am always sorry when his shrill cry fades into the distance on my homeward trail.

Back home I find his cousin, the heavenly-blue Steller's jay, shrieking across my clearing or posing picturesquely against the flame of elderberries. I am quite sure he knows how beautiful he looks there or when perched on a crimson twig of western dogwood. The jays are the most intelligent birds—barring the crows—that I have ever come across. I have often wished that we could have more of a conversation than that carried on by eye, gesture, English and jay language. He has seen a lot, that bird, and his crested black head looks as though it contained much good advice for mountain living.

Sometimes the last thing I see before going in at dusk is that other crested neighbour, the belted kingfisher. He sits on the wire cable across Teal River trying for a last fish before darkness comes quietly through my valley and climbs the high hills. Sometimes the night comes before the trout and then he leaves his perch to fly back into the underbrush beside the water. The first star comes out above Cougar and a hermit thrush murmurs sleepily.

These days and nights will live forever; the high trails and the low, the things that I have done and seen and touched and heard—and smelled and tasted. They are written down in my mind and heart and I keep going over and over them as I write, reluctant to lay any of them aside and type The End. Perhaps it is because I know there can never be any real end; not even when the earth becomes a lifeless planet spinning emptily in space and the sun which warms my valley is colder than the Teal.